◆

Oars, wheels, coir-spinning *ratts*
The songs of the shattered throat

mpT
MODERN POETRY
IN TRANSLATION

The best of world poetry

No.1 2017

© *Modern Poetry in Translation* 2017 and contributors

ISSN (print) 0969-3572
ISSN (online) 2052-3017
ISBN (print) 978-1-910485-15-6
ISBN (ebook) 978-1-910485-16-3

Editor: Sasha Dugdale
Managing Editor: Deborah de Kock
Development Manager: Sarah Hesketh
Web and Communications Manager: Ed Cottrell
Design by Jenny Flynn
Cover art by Vishwajyoti Ghosh

Printed and bound in Great Britain by Charlesworth Press, Wakefield
For submissions and subscriptions please visit www.mptmagazine.com

Modern Poetry in Translation Limited. A Company Limited by Guarantee
Registered in England and Wales, Number 5881603
UK Registered Charity Number 1118223

Supported using public funding by
ARTS COUNCIL
ENGLAND

Modern Poetry in Translation would like to thank the British Council for their
support. Translations of Monika Kumar in this issue were supported by
Literature Across Frontiers.

Songs of the Shattered Throat

CONTENTS

Focus

Reviews

Hindi poet and novelist Geet Chaturvedi wrote me a letter last year in response to my questions about the position of Hindi literature, and I was so struck by the passion of his letter that I asked if we could publish it in *MPT*. Geet's letter (pp. 81–86) describes the high status of English in India and the resulting inferiority felt by Hindi speakers and writers. I have been thinking a great deal about the relative status of languages because I translated a play by a Ukrainian playwright about the war in Donbass, a war in effect between Russian and Ukrainian speakers. She, a Ukrainian patriot, was writing in Russian, the language of the separatists and their Russian supporters, because her Russian play would be more readily translated and staged around the world and would therefore have more potency. In the same way Geet puts his elegant and thoughtful English at the disposal of his Hindi, he makes a case for Hindi's validity as a literary language in the very language that stifles it.

The Japanese novelist Minae Mizumura writes in her novel *The Fall of Language in the Age of English* that 'There is a hierarchy among languages.' All of us who are translators know intuitively about this hierarchy of languages: the way that languages, as well as currencies, are stacked against each other and ranked: hard and soft. We know that English is (for the moment) a high-status language and speaking it confers power on the speaker, we know in our heart of hearts that translating a poem into English is given a disproportionate importance, that publication in English may be valued more than publication in another language. Such a very personal disappointment, that even poetry translation does not stand outside relationships of power! To say that the Slovenian, Estonian or Afrikaans translation may reach and mean something to someone in a way the English translation or original couldn't is a correction, rather than a statement of the obvious.

Don Mee Choi, a South Korean poet and translator who has made

None of us works
in a vacuum, and
admitting that is
both a relief and
the knowledge of
a lifetime of care.

The very first issue of *Modern Poetry in Translation* is
now online at www.modernpoetryintranslation.com

her home in the United States, writes about this hierarchy in poetry and poetic essays. She calls South Korea a neo-colony of the United States, and all her translations of its poetry and literature are marked by this context: translation into the colonial language from the colonized language. She argues that it is not possible to escape the political context in translation, we live with it as we translate and it subtly acts on our selections of words, thoughts and rhythms. In her case she is giving voice to a smaller less influential literary culture in the powerful language of the dominant literary (and military) culture. To fail in this task is to be voiceless, dehumanized, but conversely the successful importing of Korean linguistic experience into English will mark English, make it expand to incorporate new works, rhythms, associations, and thereby new political possibilities, too.

In many ways Don Mee Choi's openness about geopolitical forces acting on poetry and translation is exemplary. Poetry is often allowed a purity and nobility, it can appear free-floating and distanced from the grubbier and compromising world of historical determinism and foreign policy. In part this is because it is poetry's rare ability to transcend the specific, or to work at such an oblique angle to reality that the resulting view is unrecognizable. However it would be a terrible mistake to assume that it was therefore never grounded in a specific political situation or translated into and through another.

None of us work in a vacuum, and admitting that is both a relief and the knowledge of a lifetime of care.

Sasha Dugdale

WILLIAM LANGLAND'S *PIERS PLOWMAN*

Translated by Bernard O'Donoghue

Piers Plowman was composed and revised in three principal textual forms in the last third of the fourteenth century, so it is directly contemporary with Chaucer. It was clearly a popular work because over fifty manuscripts survive. Very little is known about the author beyond some cryptic allusions in the poem itself; at one point the narrative voice says 'I have lived long in land; my name is Long Wille' and the author's name has been constructed from that. It is one of the great works of the late medieval Alliterative Revival in England, written in a pretty intelligible form of English, by contrast with the more esoteric, local alliterative language of the – also contemporary – poet of *Pearl* and *Sir Gawain and the Green Knight*.

The poem begins in a dream-vision setting, with the poet falling asleep in the Malvern Hills. But it soon becomes clear that the world in this vision is not otherworldly, but a severe scrutiny of the real world of the time. The first part of the poem is an allegorical search for a pardon from St Truth. But when this appears as a simple statement of the necessity to live a good life, the narrative changes to a search for Dowel to learn how to earn salvation. The last two-thirds of the poem consults various authoritative allegorical figures in this search. The piece printed here is part of the speech of Patience which rebukes Haukyn the Active Man for his worldliness and disregard for the plight of the poor. Passages like this one led to the poem being seen as a sociological tract up to the nineteenth century. But it is clear that Langland's concern is with social matters only as one instance of virtue. In the end, the poem's hero is Conscience who ends the poem crying out for Piers Plowman as the figure of virtue in the world.

from *Piers Plowman*

The saints' writings tell us that it's rarely seen
that God rewarded twice over any rich man.
The rich find great pleasure in their food and their dress,
and take great delight in May amongst the wild creatures
and so their joy lasts as long as it's summer.
But even at midsummer beggars go hungry,
though winter is worse for them as they go barefoot,
thirsty and hungry and shamefully insulted
and abused by rich men as is shocking to hear.
Dear Lord, send them summer and some kind of joy,
at least in Heaven, those who here had such privation
for you could have arranged it that no one was poorer,
all equally regarded and wise, if you had chosen.
Have pity for those rich folk that don't care for prisoners
because many are ungrateful for the riches you give them.
Ah God, in your mercy give them grace to amend.
For no lack will cost them more, drought or flood,
neither heat nor hail, while they have their health.
They have no shortage here of what they want and desire.
  'But poor people, your prisoners, Lord   in the depths of their misery –
comfort those creatures that feel such distress
from poverty or thirst all the days of their lives:
pain in winter for the want of clothing,
and in summer they rarely   have an adequate meal.
Comfort your wretched, Lord   in your own kingdom –
because the scriptures bear witness   how You comfort all creatures:
Turn back to me and you will be saved.

GUY VAES

Translated by Philip Mosley

Throughout his written work and photography, Guy Vaes displays an eagle eye for detail of places, especially those whose physical appearance often cues strange and unsettling experiences of a kind that may lead us beyond ordinary perception and toward a greater revelation of the world and our lives within it. A consummate flâneur, he was particularly attached to London, Edinburgh and Dublin, on which he wrote several essays celebrating their distinctive character and atmosphere. He believed those capitals to be the places most in tune with his emotional being as well as corresponding best to his aesthetic and philosophical ideas.

I was drawn to the seven poems with accompanying photos that form the suite I have translated as *The Blacktip Ragwort*. This collection may be read as a microcosmic version of his essays on those cities, but one composed in lyric verse, a literary form that he seldom practised. I was eager to discover how he expressed aspects of his identification with the cities in a manner uncommon for him. The photos date from his visits between the 1960s and 1980s, while the texts are new; the whole set having been published in a limited black-box edition following their exhibition at the Antwerp Museum of Photography in 1996. The poems take their lead from the photos but are not historically bound in any way, though 'Paternoster Row' reflects on the legacy of the *blitzkrieg* in London, and 'Westminster' is chillingly prescient in the light of the present day.

The Blacktip Ragwort

Foreword

In London, toward the middle of the Second World War, around St. Paul's Cathedral, the pink-berried willow and the yellow ragwort began to proliferate in the craters made by bombs.

Some even claimed to have numbered the blacktip ragwort there. But nothing precise allows us to support such a claim.

It's exactly because that particular variety – naïve and as if mournful symbol of disaster – was born of a collective imaginary that it emblazons this collection. For doesn't it link spontaneous storytelling to poetic expression, the defiled place to photographic properties, the dangers that lie in wait for us to our impulse to escape? Oh, so many echoes of a north where the light hasn't been able to lose its love of darkness.

Paternoster Row

(London)

The blacktip ragwort and the pink-berried willow
Besieged this place,
After the blitz and its echo of soot.

From the dome turned pyx flows out
A lake wherein to mirror the world.

Let my words be a creel.

Southwick Street

(London)

Before colours and curves
Was the straight line that nature ignores,
The white unworthily reflected by snow.

Before the Creation and its great churning
Only the sketch prevailed.

If I pondered the lesson of your design,
House in Southwick Street,
I would have the conceptual rigour
To put being and beings in their places,
I would weigh no more than a shadow
Or than my breath fused with yours
Beneath windows denying the world exists.

Westminster

(London)

On these upright chessboards
Jamaican ladies,
A king takes your rook,
Loses you a Black Angel.

There's no further opening,
Mischievous guardian of chess.
Beneath your closed eyelids
The street lets loose its bulldogs.

St. Alphege Passage

(London)

However much you challenge your shadow
In this dried-up channel where life runs its course,
It's enough that you answer to your name
(Despite yourself, of course) and all restarts in force:
The drawn-out streets, the white jellyfish suns,
The jumble of buses and, to seal it all,
The drum skin moon whose purpose you dread.

Borthwick's Close

(Edinburgh)

Outside these muted narrows
A ray of original light,

But the true Borthwick agape
At my impenetrable backward step.

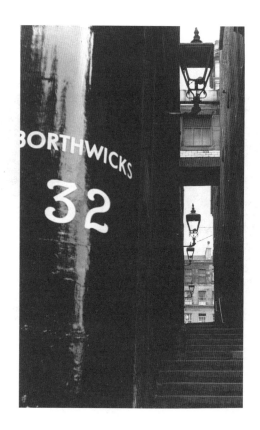

All's a Wall to Life

(Dublin)

The walls we pass through
Are more numerous than the days.
Where then did we meet one another?
In the concrete that deserves itself
Or in the clay that gives of itself?
May an annoying draft blow
Into our dull stupor,
And no grain resist us
Even when there is a snag.

Every wall precedes the world
And its crack is the illusion we project onto it.

Old Calton Burying Ground

(Edinburgh)

Time and its bagful of little treats:
If it unties the ends, a sharp obelisk falls out,
And you'll see, equally dry, embarrassed Eternity
Fading away without a single blade of grass.

KINGA FABÓ

Translated by George Szirtes

Kinga Fabó, Hungarian poet, linguist and essayist has written five
books of poetry but I didn't know her work until someone else asked
if I would translate a couple of her poems. People do occasionally
ask this – so few of us translate poetry from Hungarian after all – and
sometimes there is time, and the poems are powerful enough to
demand that at least I try. That was the case with these two poems that
immediately struck me with their vigour, virtuosity and intensity.

Both poems are about the conventional apparatus of womanhood and
presentation, mirror and girdle being associated with the process of
being appraised. It is actually the girdle that speaks in one of them:
'This sorry item, all for some man to woo or bride them.' The
promiscuous mirror is born out of the same disappointment and
fury at circumstances, but is less gendered and will wipe out any face
before it. The poems are in effect dialogues with an invisible other, racy
in diction, almost chatty but at the same time metaphysical. It is the
blend of fury and wit that determine the emotional key but it is the
form and rhyme that lend both the sharp, hard-edged, proverbial,
almost Villonesque quality I was trying to catch.

The Promiscuous Mirror

1

Is it detached or all-forgiving?
We need a passport to get through.
It nods us past in quick succession
Just anyone, no matter who.
I can rely on its detachment

As I move from place to place.
All those languages it masters,
Wherever I dare show my face!
It's no big deal who's looking in it
As it serves its own blind grace.

2

It neither befriends nor breaks up with you.
Though when you're pushed in front of it
Whether you're plain or just plain gorgeous
It frowns and takes the brunt of it.
Could this absolute indifference
Be Absolute? (It takes no joy
In my bare flesh, nor is it bored.)
In all my phases I am simply
What seems to vanish then return,
Part of its cosmic unconcern.

3

The distance is too terrifying.
It could be less but it is clear
Some speck of me would still appear.
The mirror will serve us blindly
And whether harshly or quite kindly
Forgets at once. There's little fuss,
Or major choice required for us.
It lets us do just what we want.
Mine drops me quick without a trace.
Mechanically wipes out my face.

The Complaint of a Worn-out Girdle

How many women have I tortured? God,
How many! And how perfectly deformed
their bodies were as one by one they trod

the red carpet, swayed and posed
in gratitude to me, I who prefer a closed
door to the blatantly exposed

(and they pretend to disdain me even while
seeking my good graces, S & M style)
insist I serve them with a wide-eyed smile.

Those who possess me seek the praise
– and might receive it – of the blank male gaze.
They use me and disparage me all ways

and yet are one with me, have flounced
about while in my steady grip
or slipped into me unannounced.

Talk of perverts, I am stuffed with them,
(this is where it comes to S & M).
it's like being in a prison cell.

I am the stock where these mad bats from hell
work out. I work my magic well
and turn them out as new after a spell.

They undo me, as might anyone.
I am what they have done.
But why do they insist on carrying on

with me – the feeling isn't mutual –
with me in particular.
Why pick on me when there are

plenty – women or worms – it matters not
happy to give them all they've got.
All clichés, you can stuff the lot

into one old hat and call it quits.
I'm not for clichés, not one fits.
I wish they left me alone, but it's

hopeless, I am forced to serve.
I'm always different and will swerve
from following an alien curve.

Is this their thanks? This sorry item.
All for some man to woo or bride them.
A pity it is to prettify them.

LEV OZEROV

Translated by Irina Mashinski, Maria Bloshteyn,
and Boris Dralyuk

Lev Ozerov (1914–1996), born Lev Goldberg, had a long and accomplished career as a poet, editor, and translator in the Soviet Union. He was one of the first to write about the massacre at Babi Yar, and did much to help protect and restore the reputations of authors who had suffered under Stalin, including the poets Anna Akhmatova, Boris Pasternak, and Nikolay Zabolotsky. His finest book, *Portraits Without Frames*, was published posthumously in 1999. It comprises fifty intimate, skilfully crafted accounts of encounters with some of the most important figures in Soviet culture. The book is both a testament to an extraordinary life and a perceptive mini-encyclopedia of the Soviet era. The 'portrait' below is of Ozerov's own father.

Father

He was a man with a family,
but not a family man.
A man of modest means,
he'd pack a bag and knapsack
full of bread, potatoes,
meat, a few herbs and leaves, and fruit,
and take them round to people
no one else would help.
He'd help out if someone missed their train
and had no money for another ticket.
Sometimes people took advantage;
they'd say they needed cash for a ticket

but spend it on vodka instead.
Father would come to watch
them board their trains –
and if it turned out they'd been lying,
it upset him.
'Dad, what's the matter? Are you ill?' I would ask.
Mother knew well enough,
but she'd keep quiet.
Now and again she'd grumble:
'A family, this man has a family,
but what does he care?'
Father had a special reverence for lonely old men
and insisted I revere them too.
'When you grow up... God forbid...'
He walked the streets, head held high –
chestnut curls, well-defined lips –
while all around him
lonely old men
(or men pretending to be lonely)
stumped and limped,
smacked their gums,
ducked and lisped,
minced and cowered,
moaned and groaned,
wiggled and wobbled,
cursed and fidgeted,
sniffled and trudged along.
They smelled of urine and tobacco.
Father was used to this.
He'd push his protégés into the public baths,
and they'd come out demanding beer.

'You don't need beer – you can get by on tea.'
Once a man came from Boyarka
with a young lad on his shoulders.
The boy's legs were badly deformed.
Father found a surgeon
and the boy underwent a serious operation.
One day, about fifteen years later,
I was back in Kiev on vacation
and two men dropped in for a while:
a stooped old man
and his strapping young son.
Father was invited to the wedding.
I could see no trace
in this young man
of the boy with deformed legs.
Father was always bringing back beggars,
holy fools. At first, they were quiet
and grateful, but then they'd grow brazen.
Once there was a beggar who outstayed
his welcome, a certain Timoshka,
who always ate with zest.
Chicken wings rejoiced in his hands.
Noodles went whistling through his lips –
the sound was captivating,
like a flute. He was a jealous fellow.
When father sat a colleague of Timoshka's
at the table, Timoshka quickly
finished his food,
wiped his plate clean with bread,
laid his knife, fork and spoon
neatly down on the plate,

then yelled, 'Go find yourselves
some other madman!'
and stormed out.

Father would say to me:
'What am I going to do with you?
You're a dreamer
and shouldn't be let out
into the world.
To say the world is terrible
isn't the half of it.
You look on this world,
this crazy fair,
this bloody market,
as if it were a dovecote
or an orchard.
For you, the whole earth
is a field of dandelions.
What are we going to do with you?
Your eyes are always misty,
like your mother's.
But when eyes like yours
gaze at this world's iron contours,
those contours blur and soften
into boughs of lilacs.
What are we going to do with you?
Other people become engineers,
while you just keep writing and writing...'

Tenderly, silently,
my father was ready
to take all my troubles –
present and future –
onto himself.

It's hard for me to speak
about my father. Hardest of all –
about how his life ended.
Father rushed to help
someone pleading for help
and was slain
by a gangster's bullet.
He answered the call –
he was true to himself.
Year after year I've dreamt
of blocking his path,
but I can't.

FRANCISCO FERNÁNDEZ TORRES

Translated by Róisín Tierney

I came across this poem hung on a wall in a bar in the Albaicín district of Granada, when my husband and I were there last summer. I liked it so much I just had to rush off and do a translation. It reminds me a little of Miguel Hernández's 'Nanas de la cebolla' ('Lullaby of the Onion'), and its subject lived through similar times. The author had signed the poem using a pseudonym, Arístipo, and it took me some effort over several months to make contact with him. I enlisted the help of the owner of the bar, Miguel (who kissed me on the cheek delightedly and said, '¡Lo firmo yo!' – I'll sign for it – when he realized I wanted permission to publish) and a local Flamenco dancer, Maica Molina. With their help I finally tracked him down.

Francisco Fernández Torres lives in Granada, where he worked as a teacher until his retirement. He has published two collections of poetry and is working on his third. In this poem, which is formally rhymed in the original Spanish, he writes about a local man, now deceased, who lived up in one of the caves behind Granada, near Sacramonte, the Gypsy quarter, and who had played a part in the Spanish Civil War. He was very poor, and eked out a living selling herbs and cage birds. He must have been popular, because, as well as the poem, there is a portrait of him proudly displayed on the wall of Miguel's bar.

The Desolate Goldfinch

Antonio El Moyo
carried the Republican flag.
A giant cypress, he garlanded
everyone with his friendship.

In his young fighting days
with night in his heart,
from the wall of the execution yard
in Guadix by the Darro,
between the trenches and the mud,
he set free the imprisoned song.

As tall as a bell-tower,
by trade he was a bird-seller
(canaries and goldfinches)
from his solitary cave.

On reaching his seventies
he lived off alms,
collecting wild herbs
to make healing ointments
for the fearful pains
the people suffered.

There was always a grin
between his wine-glass and his hat-brim,
a sly story always ready
in his throat.

In his cave on the Cuesta,
alone and dying,
he left this world
with only rats for company,
no family, no sandals,
no darling to cherish him.

Ay! Old friend Moyer!
In your beloved Albaicín
your friends remember you,
here in Miguel's Tavern.

LEA GOLDBERG

Translated by Rachel Tzvia Back

Lea Goldberg (1911–1970) was born in Koeningsberg, East Prussia, and spent her early years in Kovno (now Kaunas), Lithuania. Her mother tongue was Russian but already in her teens Goldberg adopted Hebrew as her language of poetic composition. After completing her doctoral studies at the University of Bonn, Goldberg emigrated to British Mandate Palestine in 1935 and lived the remainder of her life in Israel, first in Tel-Aviv and later in Jerusalem. She died of cancer at the age of 59.

In her series 'Songs of Spain', Goldberg revisits the Golden Age of Hebrew poetry (950–1492) as it emerged in Andalusia. Walking in the footsteps of Hebrew poets who flourished in Muslim and Christian Spain and established themselves there as forefathers of the Hebrew poetry tradition, Goldberg acknowledges the complex history and her own complex feelings for once-glorious Granada. There in the shadows of Alhambra's gates, poetry sang in her language, even as years later those same gates would watch over the persecution and expulsion of all Jews from its land.

Goldberg's 'Songs of Spain' are songs of love and of longing for literary landscapes Goldberg imagines herself belonging to, even as she is forever exiled from them because of generations of religious fanaticism and violence.

This series has never before been published in English. It was published in the Hebrew original in Goldberg's final poetry collection, posthumously published in 1971 and forthcoming for the first time in English under the title *On the Surface of Silence* (Hebrew Union College Press and University of Pittsburgh Press, Spring 2017).

NOTE: In the poem 'With Glory and In Poverty' the second stanza casts Granada in two contrasting biblical images of Jerusalem – the

abandoned, ash-covered and ruined city of the Book of Lamentations and the beautifully gardened city of Song of Songs. Indeed, in the third and fourth lines of the stanza, Goldberg inserts the stones and ash of Lamentations – *hayoshevet be'afar uva'even | aturat gamin* – into the well-known verse from Song of Songs that describes Jerusalem as *hayoshevet baganim* ('Thou [female] that dwellest in the gardens', Song of Songs, 8: 13). The word 'city' is gendered female in Hebrew.

Songs of Spain

1. PASSERBY

A passerby
one of many,
anonymous inheritor
of the Princes of Song –
the stake's deadly flame
burns my eyes,
and I am a tourist.

My feet touch
stone of a foreign land,
and I leaf through a list of varied names:
Ibn-Gabirol
and Góngora
and García Lorca.

2. ALL SAINTS' DAY IN TOLEDO

The blind walk by
tap-tapping
with white canes on the stone.
Girls extend their hands for alms
in clean holiday clothes –
pink and sky-blue.

Towers in the heavens
and human life on earth.

And I am both here and there,
sick with poverty,
sick with beauty.

3. ON THE ROAD TO GRANADA

Crows in the hills
as mute as the hills
and pine of the hills
black
on the ridge.

Warm earth
and cold skies.
The hills pass by in the shadow of black
birds.

Black birds
black trees.
And light on the ridge.

4. WITH GLORY AND IN POVERTY

With glory and in poverty and with the gypsies' song –
red walls and white homes
and hills dissolving into the sky.
And the bronze vessels like blood ablaze.
Bronze flowing like blood ablaze.
And a Star of David
trampled underfoot.
Bronze flowing like blood ablaze.

Your gates abandoned and no gatekeeper.
She who sits in dust and in stone
garden-embellished,
lifting smiles aloft, glowering
Granada.

5. I TALK TO YOU

I talk to you today in my tongue,
lovely-named Granada,
as though you still know my Hebrew speech,
do you not recollect –
your step-sons
and the rhythm of your gait in my tongue –
do you not recall?

Your past flutters and is smothered in my song
for who are you to me, and to you who am I?
I only saw here as I was passing by
a large white butterfly on the gates of the Alhambra.

The blood of bronze flows and roars like the lion
of my ancestors' blood in a Hebrew hymn
and your stones remembering a foreign horseman –
but who are you to me, and to you who am I?
I only saw here as I was passing by
a large white butterfly
on the gates of the Alhambra.

MARINA TSVETAEVA

Translated by Moniza Alvi and Veronika Krasnova

Josef Brodsky considered Marina Tsvetaeva the most important Russian and European poet of her generation and the sincerest of Russian poets. In spite of the extreme hardship of her life in Russia after the Revolution and then abroad she possessed an extraordinary self-discipline and worked every day. Thus her lyric poems can be read as diary notes and provide a glimpse into her personality and her state of mind at a certain period of time.

The poems we translated here were written in the mid-thirties. In a few years (in 1939) Tsvetaeva – against her better judgement – would return to the Soviet Union, following her husband and daughter. In 1935–36 she spent two summers in France on a small farm in the Savoie. It was a rare, peaceful interlude in her otherwise predominantly urban life.

The intonation of these poems is light and vibrant. Accompanying her on her travails streams, trees and flowers become participants in her complex philosophy of art and the artist's role in the world. She conveys the hardship of a poet's lot, as well as its catharsis.

This is the second group of Tsvetaeva's poems that we translated and we were getting a clearer sense of how we might render in English her powerful, uncompromising voice and her tonal range. Sometimes we translated the poems into a more flowing English initially, and then reduced them to a more honed or terser style. After our initial discussions and deliberations, translating the poems was a joy although 'A Poet's Fate', with its intricacy of argument played out across five stanzas, took a long time to settle.

To a Young Poet

Again and again –
dogged by thoughts of you
poppy after poppy
I behead the whole garden.

Likewise in a parched summer
at the field's edge
death's casual hand
will pluck off my head.

From the Train

The icy tiara of the mountains –
for a human life, just a frame.

Today I parted the ivy
on a castle's granite wall.

Today on all the roads
pine trees streamed behind me.

Today I held a tulip
by the chin, like a child...

The Apple Tree

. . . so, nothing at all for me
in return for the banquet I've given.

Ah, after the long winter
the apple tree freely
bestows her blossom.

The Stream

I glimpse my heart reflected in the water.

Am I following the stream, or is it following me?
We must both make our own way
rippling over the unfeeling stones, singing their praises.
We have no power on earth to shift them.

I flow with the current –
or is the stream hurrying to keep up with me,
its wave curving like a swimmer's shoulder?

Wherever we find a stream
a poet is nearby!

Lucky people, shedding tears
pouring them into us both
so they can feel better,
then rinsing their tear-stained faces.

All the water clouded
by their past sorrows!
We carry this sadness forever
so they are able to forget.

Certainty

Looking up into the blue sky
you exclaim – there'll be thunder!

Raising your eyebrows at a rogue
you're certain – you'll fall in love!

Through the indifference of grey moss
I proclaim – there will be poems!

A Poet's Fate

How blessed they are,
those who are unable to sing!
Their tears flow – what a relief it must be
for grief to pour down like rain.

There's a shuddering
under the heart's stone.
Commanded to sing among the graves,
to be born a poet is my cruel fate.

David sang a lament for Jonathan
even though he was broken in two.
If Orpheus hadn't descended into hell
he could have sent his voice,

his voice alone gone down into the dark
while he stood at the threshold
allowing Eurydice to walk right out
on the tightrope of his song.

A rope-walk into the day.
Blinded by light – she couldn't look back.
I know if you're given a poet's voice
all the rest will be taken from you.

JÁN GAVURA

Translated by James Sutherland-Smith and the poet

In Gavura's work the poetic persona has a strong empathy with nature, seeing it as an example of both a non-human otherness and as part of God's creation. As a theologian Gavura regards nature and humanity as part of a post-lapsarian existence. Gavura's natural world and the animals which inhabit it are true to themselves and the savagery they express is an aspect of the innocence they retain. His poems draw on everyday feelings of doubt, fear, disillusionment, anger, weakness or even evil thoughts and he tries to bring together these aspects of the contingent world and gain insight. Given his religious sensibility Gavura's poems frequently incorporate a mythical dimension. This spiritual bedrock in Gavura's poetry paradoxically opens his poetry to all readers with its acute positioning of human beings, nature and divine aspiration.

An Intake of Breath

So far you've chosen where you want to wait,
but can't choose whether to wait or not.

From the bowl on the table you taken the biggest piece of fruit,
but hunger is not easy to calm, as if you warn a child
with a threat, a glance or refusal to touch.

You think of three names at once,
from the Hebrew, Russian and Latin past
you choose the Roman modesty of the word *paulus*.

During one untimely December twilight, broken with dread
you see a being so akin to you.
The child, you quieten, doesn't heed your threats. Or looks.

The hand that stretches out unwittingly,
is a greeting of welcome, a plea of the drowning.

Your North

It's snowing and for the first wind
with the taste of sea foam
a man comes out of the house.
The eternal November brings
a message from an icy desert, where only the pure survive.

You come out after him,
wrapped only in a sheepskin coat, you shove to the front
the big girl with dark eyes,
and the smaller one with eyes like yours.
Before the moon turns around at full,
You'll give birth for the third time.

But in the man's voice something growls, the north.
And the wind won't stop speaking,
it rustles in the memory, asks questions. Where and when.

The surface is broken by cold, fear by desire,
polar light by awakening. You are. Here. With him.

Never wholly yours,
your man. He won't leave today.

In Absentio

The only building without a number
in Cemetery Street is the House of Hope.

For the quiet trees on the rocks above
something unbelievable happens.
From all sides people come
for somebody, who is no longer here.

A man and dog mount the steep path
without noticing that the effort purifies their blood.
On traces of the early snow they find
their own footprints, in a bush the wing of a hawk.
The bird not.

You walk out from a dry circle round a tree,
frozen snow crackles like snow,
not like broken glass. From below sounds
a song in a dead language.

Participation

To hunt a roe deer means to yank it down,
to shove its long neck into the rain-soaked clay and to trip
its legs, suddenly uncertain with blood, which
splay like spillikins.

Oh, how many nightly absent events, what games.

In the morning, among herbs, a head is placed
on the ground stretched like an altar cloth,
while the rest of the body of the deer jiggles
in the bellies of all the jackals around.
Communal Supper of a Sacred Hare

In the first scenario it was a fox that caught
the spoor of a hare fresh enough to be worth following
and waiting for a gust of wind.

Before the hare got to an asphalt road,
its neck was broken and its body chilled.

In a different scenario it was an eye of a hen eagle
that glimpsed the hare's shadow. On a cropped field by the road
the hare's senses stood no chance.

Hungrily but carefully the fox strips flesh from the back legs.
From the other side with spread wings the bird of prey
gulps down the intestines.

They have no time to notice the road or cars.
the hare is already half-consumed,
incisor teeth and the hook of a beak come closer together.
They ascend the white ribs as if upon a staircase.

NURDURAN DUMAN

Translated by Karen McCarthy Woolf

In summer 2015 I was Poet in Residence at the National Maritime Museum. This led me to consider my own relationship with water, the sea and most locally the River Thames. My first collection *An Aviary of Small Birds* was a book of elegies, through which I discovered an enduring preoccupation with how being on, in or near water made me feel different. This is a strand I've continued to explore in my new collection *Seasonal Disturbances*: at its centre is a long poem, 'Conversation, With Water', written on board a Dutch barge opposite the Houses of Parliament, in a Japanese form called a 'zuihitsu', which, in its prose/poetry hybrid Duman's poem 'The River' resembles. The fact that I wrote this poem while *on* the water is significant as the 'experiential' poetics that underpin its creation are in part how Nurduran Duman and I first met. As part of the residency I ran a number of workshops; one of which started at the National Poetry Library at the Southbank. We then walked across Hungerford Bridge, writing haiku along the way, before catching the Thames Clipper downriver to Greenwich Pier. Nurduran, who trained as a maritime engineer, was visiting from Istanbul and signed up out of curiosity, on the advice of the Poetry Library – which was something of an honour given her reputation and profile in Turkey! On the boat I asked students to write journal notes, documenting their response to the feeling of being on the water; once we arrived at the National Maritime Museum we worked on poems again, this time in response to paintings and historical artefacts. After class Nurduran and I visited another type of watering hole (aka The Pub!) and in the spirit of the moment, and of Nurduran, who has an infectious dynamism and energy, we decided to start work on a translation, using her literal as a starting point. Nurduran has an extremely focused, bell-like clarity to her work, and this, I hope, is what this translative collaboration captures.

The River

Is it the bird's rush
or do the clouds dance?
The surface is frosted glass.

Listen! The sounds are building their bridge in the lunar park;
between yesterday and later, from words to frou-frous. The sounds
take their places – in the water, on trees; recorded forever in space as
radio waves. We have the ability not to listen. But if we listen we do
not have to hear.

The city's getting taller.
Yellows flow with the boat,
birds hit windows.

This city loves its clouds, but clouds aren't the bad guy in this life
story. Neither is the sun, even though it takes days to break through.
Does the sun's smile have a sound?

Stained glass love is restored
waiting for the wind's tune.
Paper ships flutter on roofs.

ANN JÄDERLUND

Translated by Johannes Göransson

Ann Jäderlund's *Som en gång varit äng* (Which once was meadow) is one of the seminal texts of modern Swedish poetry. When it was published in 1988 it provoked a heated discussion in Swedish media (the so-called 'Ann Jäderlund Debates') because of the way it challenged many prevailing aesthetic norms in Swedish literary culture. On the one hand, these experiments were similar to the ones that were taking place in US poetry at the time – the fragmented syntax, the sense of obscurity, the use of collage – but in radical contradistinction to the anti-poetic, modernist rhetoric of US models of avant-gardism, Jäderlund's necropastoral invocations of flowers and romantic love harkened back to pre-modernist traditions, frequently directly collaging medieval ballads. Perhaps most importantly: in contradistinction to the US avant-garde model which valorizes critical distance, Jäderlund's poetry is feverishly visceral in its explorations of love and violence. However, the book works cumulatively, as the short, often elliptical poems gradually lead the reader into a saturated, dramatic and heightened space. The task of any Jäderlund translator is to maintain this intensity while at the same time juggling the often ambiguous valences caused by fragmented syntax and the mere hints of an almost opaque narrative. Since the publication of *Meadow*, Jäderlund has continued to write and publish, her poetry continuing to influence Swedish poets (for example Aase Berg and Helena Boberg), and is widely recognized as one of the most important Swedish poets of the last 50 years. Jäderlund has also written for the stage, and in 2013 she published a collection of her translations of Emily Dickinson, *Gång på gång är skogarna rosa*.

The Imperial Hotel

It was like heavy grapes in my heavy head
It was in the moss where one opened the capsule
It was his soft fingers across the veins of the blade
It was in the blood where one dips blood

Maria Rose

We tortured a rose and the rose's origin
I pressed your knee against the middle of the rose
You stood up my breast-leaves fell out of the side
Over the other rose which grew strong and white

A Hamlet Cabinet

It is a deposit
His pupils widen

But are coloured back in
To that and that

Is it elements
I do not collapse

It is a gift in a cabinet
But does he ever give the gift

It is a gift but is it his eyes
Or outside the reach of the cabinet

For every time when he has walked far behind
It glows on me still

Venus De Milo

Here I have no arms
Don't pull out a shell I have

Here I have no eyes
Can it bind my eyes

Do not pull back the veil
Is it a snail can it stiffen

A Veil

The small breast-leaves
Move in his fluid

White is not my fluid
The pistils pull together

Nevermore will it blossom
It has never blossomed

Perforate him

Underchamber

Pick me apart again
I am after all no chamber

When I myself try
To pick myself apart

I cannot see
They are big cores

A Strong Tenderness

I opened your hand with my hands
You pushed one finger down in my brown throat
I burnt you until you became warm too
In my breast in my throat in the well
We struck against the flats they did not weaken
I pressed your style against the well's sorrow
It is a sorrow well now it releases me
In this strong well which falls

SONGS OF THE SHATTERED THROAT

Focus on the Languages of India

TULSIDAS

Translated by Rohini Chowdhury

Tulsidas, the most important of the saint-poets of the medieval Bhakti movement in northern India, is also Hindi's most renowned poet and his magnum opus, the *Ramcharitmanas*, is unanimously regarded as the greatest achievement of Hindi literature. Tulsi's retelling of the story of Ram – written in the vernacular Awadhi, between the years 1574 and 1576–77 – had instant popular appeal. Within a very short time, Tulsi's *Ramayana*, carried by wandering sadhus, recited and performed across towns and villages, had spread across northern India. Today, more than 400 years since its composition, the *Ramcharitmanas*, sung, recited or performed, remains an essential part of the religious, cultural and social landscape of northern India. The work consists of 12,800 lines (which exactly double in number in translation into English) divided into 1073 stanzas, mainly in the chaupaai and doha metres, and set in seven 'kands' or cantos.

The following stanzas (nos. 232 and 233, from 'Childhood', the first canto of the great epic *Ramcharitmanas*) describe Sita's first encounter with Ram – they run into each other, by accident, in the king's flower garden, where Ram and his younger brother Lakshman have gone to admire the garden and collect flowers for their morning worship, and where Sita has come, accompanied by her companions, to offer worship at the temple of the goddess Girija. Sita, hearing that the two princes were in the garden, and having heard of their great fame and beauty, goes with her friends to steal a look at them. Seeing Ram, Sita is overcome by love and shuts her eyes, and one of her companions, bolder than the rest, then describes the two brothers to her.

Rohini Chowdhury's complete translation of Tulsidas's *Ramcharitmanas* will be published by Penguin Random House India as a Penguin Classic in 2019; this excerpt has been used with the publisher's permission.

Two Stanzas from 'Childhood'

Sita, bewildered, was looking all around her
'Where have the young princes gone?' she worried.
Wherever the fawn-eyed Sita turned her glance,
Quantities of shining white lotuses rained down.
Her companions then pointed out, hidden behind some vines
The handsome youths, one dark, the other fair.
Seeing his beauty, her eyes were filled with longing,
And she rejoiced as though she had found her own treasure.
With unwavering gaze she looked upon Raghupati's radiance,
Her very eyelids forgot to blink.
In the intensity of her love, she lost all sense and awareness of her body
Like a chakor bird gazing at the autumn moon.
Through the pathway of her eyes she took Ram into her heart
Then wisely shut the doors of her eyelids.
When her companions realised that Sita was overcome by love,
They were abashed and could not say a word.

From the arbour of creepers and vines,
Emerged at that very moment, the two brothers,
Like two radiant moons
Through a curtain of clouds.

'The two handsome brothers are the very pinnacles of beauty,
Their bodies are as bright and splendid as the blue lotus and the golden.
Elegant peacock feathers, entwined with bunches of flowerbuds here and there
Adorn their heads.
Upon their foreheads gleam their tilaks and drops of perspiration,
Their ears are adorned with beautiful ornaments,
With curving eyebrows, and curly hair,
And eyes as bright as new lotus buds,
And handsome chin and nose and cheeks
And charming smiles that captivate the heart –
The radiance of their faces is such that I cannot describe it:
Beholding them puts innumerable gods of love to shame.
Jewelled necklaces upon their breasts, conch-like necks
And arms strong and powerful, like the trunk of Love's young elephant.
And the one with the cup of leaves full of flowers in his left hand –
The dark prince, my dear – is utterly enchanting.

Slim-waisted as a lion, clad in yellow garments
He is the abode of beauty and grace.'
Beholding the jewel of the solar dynasty,
Sita's companions forgot themselves completely.

KUTTI REVATHI

Translated by Vivek Narayanan, Padma Narayanan
and the author

Kutti Revathi is in a long tradition of a certain kind of woman poet in
India, writing in a number of languages, whose poems are at once
intensely cerebral, intellectual, allusive and fearlessly erotic. In
her case, she is deeply immersed in the linguistics, history and heritage
of the Tamil language, not least through her study of its traditional
medicine. Her vocabulary turns the poem into a far echo chamber – as
perhaps ought to be natural for a thoroughly modern poet working in a
language with a two-thousand-year-old unbroken literary tradition.
Nevertheless, ironically, even a 'native' Tamil reader can find some of
the poems difficult, not only for their sometimes obscure vocabulary,
but because they can be suddenly discontinuous and full of powerful
obliquities. She first became famous in Tamil public life when a
poem from her second book, *Mulaigal* (Breasts) was attacked for its
supposedly pornographic content by leading male film lyricists and
poets. While the poem faced an extended public debate and excoriation
in magazines and on TV talk shows, the writer herself faced violent
threats and obscene phone calls. This only proves true the idea that,
as Rilke says somewhere, 'fame is nothing more than the sum of
misunderstandings that gather around a [person's] name'; in fact the
poem was not explicit at all in the usual sense. Revathi has said she
wanted to explore women's breasts as 'inhabited reality' and not
'exhibited commodity'; but again, it is also important for us to know
that her word for 'breasts', *mulaigal*, reaches back to the vocabulary of
the Sangam era, the earliest, most ancient strata of Tamil poetics.
   The making of this translation involved three people – Padma, who
is a fully bilingual translator of Tamil prose; Revathi who lives and
dreams much more in Tamil but also speaks an English that is excellent
and more than adequate to both everyday and academic conversation;

and Vivek, who grew up speaking Tamil and can read the script, but whose reading of the written language is hobbled at best. Usually, Vivek begins by discussing the poem with Padma, who makes the first trot, and then closely, going line by line, with Revathi. Vivek sits down to copy out the poem and make one or several drafts of it in English, then takes it back to Revathi. The two of them then decide the final form of the poem in English.

Nakedness

For you me her
nakedness is the glittering weapon
When wet with blood's sweat
it attains the perfection of its training
As trees reach their nakedness they
turn wing-sprouting birds
The Chinese soldiers used to say
Don't ever draw
your sword from the sheath
  without a reason
It isn't easy to live with nakedness
When it grows and grows
like a flame from the fire
it will torment you
But don't ever draw
your sword unnecessarily
  searching for the chance to use it
Even if it should rust and turn into a sieve
Keep it with you
Make it your own

She, a Lotus Pond

All across her buds of dew come up
I'll make every single bud a fruit
pluck it unbroken with my tongue
like the water brushing up the banks
her heaving heart-breaths
against the chest those waves rolling over
the palms opened wide
her navel like a leaf's
depression radiated outwards...
Like a parrot with a piece of fruit in its beak
she offers it, her body
leads and lends it to my lips we drink each other like ecstatic tea
sinking in her smoky hair
disoriented gasping for air
her scattered footsteps on the floor are branches
Going into the water
with a snake's slippery speed
having with heavy rainy thighs come running
we make it in the flowering mud one to the other
I'm circling her beehive with my busy breath
And then every day at dawn the four breasts
smile like lotus blooms

Chimera

your intoxicated eyes
pour into me
a great blood-waterfall
my bones' hissing tide

they want to touch and taste
my glances do
grafting into you
history's shoots

your words
brimming in me
silent at my base
curling

you tear
the quiet in two
all over me
strike rain

later on the hardened floor
the sound of those heavy drops falling
for a long while...
season following season
time dragged on
sobbing for freedom
it brought me back

your words
brimming in me
at my base curled up quietly

Explosives

The cycles of the body that women
turn into explosives
keeping them hidden inside
And when they can't anymore handle
the stench of the bomb-powder or the radiating heat
they open those bodies up
In the rains
getting sodden
they sprout from those bombs like seeds
Time stretches out in the seasons
In the summers again
breathing in the loneliness and the radiating heat
getting ready to blow
pouring through the changing light
of so many rooms
to the last one's soft glow
That explosive's fuse
when she touched it with her desire
body in little pieces
blasts and scatters
In all the organs
explosives kept hidden
and in their uteruses and in their breasts
like fruits, rotting

K.G. SANKARA PILLAI

Translated by Aditya Shankar

This poem was originally written in Malayalam by K. G. Sankara Pillai (often credited as KGS), a poet from Kerala, India. He is one of the pioneers of new-left modernism in Malayalam poetry and he came to public notice in the early 1970s with the publication of his poem 'Bengal'. As critics in India have often observed, justice is the core of his poetic vision. His writing, a critique of the deep state, is a new form of writing the nation. The poems of KGS are driven by the quest for human rights and by environmental issues. He pioneers and takes part in resistance movements, and his avant-garde poetry has been widely used as a tool for popular movements and protests.

The poem here, 'The River Discards its Name at the Sea', is a modern hymn to love from a land of honour killings. The poem is a dialogue between the corpses of two lovers. The river and its two banks represent the two castes that force the lovers apart. When the river reaches the limitless ocean, it represents the liberation of love and lovers from the narrowness of social hierarchy. In a caste-driven society, inter-caste love often attains fruition through death. Hence, the poem uses the metaphor of corpses engaged in a dialogue in their journey towards the sea. The corpses, Anandan and Mathangi, are characters from Buddhist tales.

The River Discards its Name at the Sea

At the dock
near the court,
the corpse
floating downstream
spoke to a dangling corpse:

Mathangi,
come down,
let's bathe.

See,
Sunlight swims,
kissing on the
lips of water, and
listening to the
movie soundtrack.

Come down,
let's float
in this passionate chill.

The demon of water
will not separate us
into two worlds
of well and light.

The love of the dead
will not be punished
by caste and religion.

No more
the moderation of love,
the restraint within boundaries,
the mugginess of hermitage,
or coping with sadness.

No more
the whiplash of morality
on our greedy senses,
salvation in faith,
the kind face of justice in knowledge –

Mathangi, no more
any of these, in death.
Do you see
the estuary where the cranes sunbathe?

Do you see
the English school,
the sad fort
that hasn't forgotten
Nargis-Raj Kapoor
film posters, and
the party office and
caste office where
idol worship is celebrated?

If you pass these
and a couple of stares,
you will reach the sea.

The river discards
its name at the sea.
Land is left behind.

Like love, the river
will keep flowing.
Those sea waves hold the
frequented routes of love.

Come down,
let's travel
as a pair of waves.

Swaying in the river wind,
Mathangi said:

Now that
you came, Ananda,
do not cover your love,
like nudity, in spiritual robes,
do not be thirst-crazy
under stress.

For me,
you are the sea;
a sea without any other shore.

ED DOEGAR

The *Ainkuṟunūṟu* is one of the eight anthologies of Classical Tamil verse. Commissioned by a king in the early decades of the third century CE, '*Ainkuṟunūṟu*' literally means 'the Short Five Hundred'. The text contains 500 *akam* (love) poems which are divided into five sections each containing 100 poems and dealing with a different aspect of love. These sections were individually authored by a poet considered a virtuoso in each style. These various aspects of love are named after flowers or plants that grow in a particular landscape which serves as the section's setting; so 'marutam verses', which concern the (male) lover's unfaithfulness, are named after the marutam plant (queen's flower) and are located in the agricultural lowlands. Each landscape setting (*tiṇais*) is populated with a complex symbolic ecosystem of tropes, figures and gestures. The richness of the symbolic allegory means that the actions of the characters are sometimes wholly implied through images of the natural world, for instance a lover's infidelity might be seen in a vine's creeping grasp. This formal constraint is contrasted by an extreme urgency of address. The poems are dramatic and the characters' speak to each other, albeit obliquely, with forceful intensity.

The paradoxical nature of the poems, at once feeling-ful but restrained, sensually immediate yet contextually remote, presents a problem for translation; all the more so as I don't read Tamil, classical or modern. In preparing these versions I have relied entirely on the work of other translators, principally the scholars A. K. Ramanujan and Martha Ann Selby, to provide the source text. Though both these translators have created excellent reading versions of the *Ainkuṟunūṟu* their versions vary substantially and it is in this difference that I glimpse my own version of the *Ainkuṟunūṟu*. For means of comparison, here is the first verse of the sequence I have called 'In Riverside Cane', Martha Ann Selby renders it:

Shamed by the cruelty
of the man from the riverbank
where the purslane creeper planted in the house
coils around a reed,
we will say that he is good.

Our soft, round shoulders contradict us.

Whereas A K Ramanujan offers this:

Green creepers planted inside the house
twine themselves with the cane outside
in his country of rivers.

Embarrassed
by his careless cruel ways, we say,
'He's a good man,'

but my round soft arms
say, 'Not so, he's not,'
and grow thin.

My version of this verse follows this introduction and demonstrates
the liberties I have allowed myself throughout the sequence.

The first two excerpts are presented as they appear in the original
text. They are a series of dramatic expressions themed around a
central metaphor or circumstance. 'In Riverside Cane' is spoken by
the heroine as she considers her lover's infidelity. 'What They Say To
Him' is voiced by the heroine's confidantes who address and rebuke
the hero for his dalliance with a pubescent rival. The final sequence,

'From The *Ainkuṟunūṟu*', is a composite piece, taking a single verse
from each section of the anthology.

What They Say To Him

Eight Neytal Poems after Ammūvaṉār

1

That's her, isn't it? Your little friend ...
She likes to make a bit of a splash, doesn't she?
Look at her braids, getting drenched in the sea.

2

There she is again, your sweetheart!
Asking the seagulls to find that necklace
You lent her. The one she lost in the sand.

3

Who's that? Oh look, it's that kitten of yours
Making such a fuss of a few cold waves!
Listen to her friends shriek at each slap.

4

Didn't we see her – your intended that is –
Throwing fistfuls of mud at the sea
Because it ruined her pretty sand-palaces?

5

Bit highly strung, that darling of yours,
We saw her kohled eyes turn all cloudy red
As the sea snatched her sand-dollies away.

6

A picture of innocence, your chosen one.
Bees swarm to such dark rimmed eyes!
Watch her wade into the swell to escape them!

7

Isn't she restrained, your delicate petal...
Those jewels of sweat on your chest won't wet
The nettle-flowers she wears at her breast.

8

Such a sweet game your little friend plays
Pressing the milkless bud of her breast
To the suckless lips of her favourite doll.

In Riverside Cane

Five Marutam Verses after Ōrampōkiyār

1

The vine we planted for the house
               Has spread
It leeches onto anything
Gripping the thin reeds by the river.

He's a cruel man.

                                   My soft round shoulders

Say nothing

As I insist   He's a good man.

2

He knows his rivers

                 Every shaded grove

He knows where the cane is high enough

Where the white blooms

                 Like the tufts of a horse's mane

                       Sway gently, a curtain.

 Even at midnight

                           When everything's still

                           In the sleepy villages

Those country girls get no rest.

3

                 Where the blossom of the reeds

Tangles with the new growth

                 Of that neighbouring mango tree

You'll find his broad bare chest

                 Offering itself as a bed.

4

             The floods bring the riverbed fresh grit.

Girls

         With nothing on their minds

                      Except

          A pretty dress

          Come

To bathe
With their companions
The tall-standing sugar cane.

His whole life
He has spent here
In this ancient town

He belongs to us
But doesn't.

5

In the shadowed groves

Where the reeds grow
And scentless flowers reach
To thread their fingers through
The mango tree

On the thicker branches
The smell lingers
Of lovers' bodies
The sweet and sour
Of excitement.

My eyes burn
Tears peel like petals in the rain.

From the Ainku_runū_ru

To her confidante

I have to tell you, listen ...

Sweeter than milk
   Tempered with honey
      Gathered from our highest garden

Is the ditch water
   That drains from his fields
      In gullies covered with dry leaves

Used only by animals.

To himself

Pitiless summer
Unbearably bright
This land
Devoured by wildfire
Is ash and emptiness

But if I only close my eyes
Here she is

My precious copper-skinned girl
Arms freckled with gold
Sudden as kino flowers

Her hair
Quick and slow
As dripping honey

There
On that cool balcony
In the dark thick night.

To her confidante

The sea – his sea – fills the conch with its song ...
                    Oh, listen to me!
Do fishermen fear the heave and crash
Of the ocean they send themselves into?

How can I hide
                    How my bangles slips from my wrist
When he leaves

                    How they tighten on his return?

To her confidante

The vine we planted for the house
                    Has spread
It leeches onto anything
Gripping the thin reeds by the river.

He's a cruel man.

                    My soft round shoulders
Say nothing
As I insist   He's a good man.

                              To her

                    In the peacock's dance
                         You danced

                    Deer would startle
                         As you do

                And just as your knit brow
                         Opens
                    The jasmine bloomed

                    Full of thoughts of you
                    Of your lineless face
                         I have run
                    Faster than the rains.

KUNWAR NARAIN

Translated by Apurva Narain

Kunwar Narain combines a modern international sensibility with a grounding in India's cultural history, and some of his poems traverse multiple terrains. The two poems published here illustrate this well. They are international in context, yet deeply personal, transposing experiences from over half a century ago into today's milieu; and this movement in time and space is made within a deceptively simple linguistic construct. The 'experiment' is conducted not in the lurid exteriors of the poems but in their inner recesses, resonating after them – this is a technique that the poet's later work sometimes employs, and it represents a challenge for the translator.

'Warsaw 1955, with Nâzim Hikmet' recalls an experience of formative literary importance for the poet – when he, then a young man, spent time with writers like Neruda, Hikmet and Słonimski among others, in a long trip through post-war Europe, Russia and China.

In these poems, the long gestation period between the event and the poem is not just reminiscent of the poet's own unhurried hesitant world but is also a geographical and temporal continuum across which a particular past acquires relevance today in some universal reinvention of itself. Both poems are from the collection *Hāshiyé Kā Gawāh* (Witness in the margin), published in 2009.

Warsaw 1955, with Nâzim Hikmet

He had come from Moscow to Warsaw
The fatigue of Turkey's prison-life
was still fresh on his face

I remember a restaurant
near a church that is now
quiet like a mystery,
a gathering of writers
where for the first time
and then many times
I had met Hikmet

I remember his heavy, coarse, rustic hands
on my hands, my knees,
when he made a point
enthusiastically...

I do not remember all he said
but I remember well
the poet's persona
which had then filled
another poet's early life
with its boundless love of life

Time changes, views change, places change,
but a poet's solicitudes
do not change so much

The remembrance of a casual meet
even today
makes life more complete

Guernica

'I paint objects as I think them, not as I see them.'
– Picasso

It is arduous
to restore in a painting
a mangled face
as it was before,
to piece together
the broken bits bit-by-bit
and re-create it
exactly as it was.

It is better to demolish the remains
and create something new
    from the rubble...

An eye was saved
in it some light
in the light some signs of life

In the teeth sticking to the lips
there was still stuck a laughter
    child-like

In the tattered geography of the face
the ten percent nook for the mind
between two ears open like windows
    was disconcerting

The nose could be pulled and straightened
up to the length of the tongue
    but not raised

The rest of the body
was that mauled-up mess under the head
that instead of being put right in its place
    could be put from any to any place.

All in all
the unquiet map that emerged
    could be of a human being
    or of the world.

Hindi Medium Type

English here in India is not just any language but a language that signifies status and one-upmanship. Sure, it is a language of communication in many cities and a means of employment. But it is also a matter of a superiority complex. Concomitantly, the vernacular is often looked down upon. Everywhere, in schools, corporates, government offices, we are told: 'Even if you write poorly, write in English. It will make an impression. If it is in Hindi, even when extraordinary, nobody will pay heed, neither the manager, nor the officer, nor the government, nor the media.'

I worked for twelve years in the largest media house of this country which publishes the largest circulated Hindi daily, and I have seen it there, too. The employees were asked repeatedly to write all communication, either in-house or external, in English. The reason? It will improve the company's brand image. I still remember the words: 'Although we produce a Hindi newspaper, we don't work in Hindi because we don't want to encourage the "Hindi psyche". What we communicate is what we think. We want our people to think in English, but make a product that is in Hindi.' And it is true with almost every sector. Bollywood makes Hindi movies but behind the scenes, they work in English. Hindi TV, one of the biggest industries, produces Hindi serials but it works in English. The bureaucrats, the politicians, the policy makers, all think and work in English. English is the language of the 'successful' people.

In government offices, applications in English move faster. Even if you are highly educated in Hindi, if you don't know English, your chances of employment are bleak. Even for the post of a Hindi teacher in the Hindi-speaking belt of India, fluency in English is a requisite.

This is a situation which has filled the Hindi-speaking people with a kind of inferiority, discontent and a kind of shameful annoyance towards Hindi, and English also. And this is reflected in everything, in their psyche, in their lifestyle, in their thinking. I have watched this 'Hindi-won't-give-you-any-success' notion very closely. In my adolescence, I saw a friend of mine beaten brutally by his father in a city like Mumbai. His crime: he was reading a Hindi literary novel. It triggered his father's ire, 'Why are you reading Hindi? If you really want to read a book that is not in your school curriculum, read an English novel. At least, it will improve your English. It will help you get a job. Hindi won't give you anything.' His father who was very good in Hindi, but had very little English himself, had faced many problems in his life because of his ignorance of English. According to him, his poverty and failures were directly related to his 'not-knowing-English'. His father resembles many fathers in my country. This was twenty years ago and the situation is no better now.

The majority in India see people who work, write and speak in English achieve every kind of success. What has this resulted in? A widespread infatuation with English. It has created a society without pride in its own language. At a very subtle level, India is going through a very idiosyncratic linguistic problem, almost unseen at the surface but working at the psychological level. A linguistic class struggle. A problem which is a by-product of the colonial legacy and its fossils.

It has fostered a few generations perfect in neither Hindi nor English. Nor are they much into literature. But thanks to them, it has become a widespread perception that whatever is in Hindi, literature or other, is no good. They watch Hindi films, sing Hindi songs, but for them, reading books in Hindi (or any other Indian language) is not a great idea because Hindi books are no good. Needless to say people prefer a language that gives them a sense of pride and money. Hindi media has helped to increase this perception. One doesn't find Hindi book reviews even in Hindi newspapers. Their columnists are not Hindi writers. They are English writers whom the newspaper translates into Hindi and publishes on their editorial page everyday. The Hindi papers publish reviews of English books only because 'the stuff in Hindi is not good'. Yet they think they themselves are 'good', albeit Hindi. It sounds like a joke.

This perception deters many from taking Hindi seriously. The books and their writers don't get the respect they deserve. This linguistic tussle of superiority and inferiority, Hindi psyche and English psyche is evident in the term 'HMT'. HMT used to be the most popular brand of wristwatches in India. But now this acronym has a different connotation. English-speaking elitists began to use it to ridicule and deride the Hindi speakers by calling them 'HMT' or 'Hindi Medium Type', the people who received their education in Hindi medium schools. 'Oh come on! Don't take him seriously, he's just an HMT.'

What can we hope for when a language and its people face so much disrespect? How many translators will a language attract when it faces a crisis amongst its own readership? How to fight this perception that 'if it is in Hindi, it is not good'? It automatically connects with the writer. I have heard it many times, 'Oh that man? He writes in Hindi, is he any good?'

This has turned Hindi literature into a ghetto, an inferior kind of ghetto, though this ghetto is greater than many other ghettos in this country. This inferiority has its own superiority complex, a rather peculiar one.

◆

In India, there is almost no institutional or academic support for translation. Most translations are done voluntarily. People start by translating a couple of poems by a poet, do another ten to fifteen poems and then stop. Mostly the translators are poets themselves, either English or Hindi, and at some stage they feel that it would be better to concentrate on their own poetry instead of translating others. I haven't seen a Miłosz or Ted Hughes working here. Miłosz was a celebrated bilingual, he spent a great deal of time translating others. I remember he was known in the US primarily as Zbigniew Herbert's translator until the mid 70s. Ted Hughes worked hard on other people's literal versions, published and promoted them widely. I don't find such dedication here, although India has many great bilinguals. In the last two decades, use of English has increased and it has, in fact, increased the possibilities of translation into English. In the last five years, every major Indian publisher has published books in English translations, but they are primarily for the Indian audience. Most of these translations don't cross borders. The European and the US markets show no interest in these titles.

Here is another thing – there is a strong sense of disapproval for Indian translators in the West. I have heard many people saying Indian translators don't have 'an ear' for writing in English. They translate in an English that is fine for the Indian audience but not the West. I don't know how many Indian translators have submitted for the PEN Translation award, but in the 13-year history of PEN/Heim Translation Awards, only two Indian translators have been recognised, Arvind Krishna Mehrotra, a poet himself (in 2009, for his translations of Kabir, a medieval Hindi poet) and Anita Gopalan for her translation of my work of fiction, *Simsim*. The PEN award win has made Anita Gopalan a big inspiration for the Hindi literary world as I have seen many younger people taking up the challenge to translate Hindi writers into English after her win.

If you look at the archives of literary journals available online, Hindi (or any other Indian language) barely registers. Hindi is the fourth most widely spoken language in the world, but I have never seen any Hindi writer making headlines in European or US publishing. Let's leave that aside (since they don't make it even in India), I seldom find Hindi authors in western magazines.

What my language needs is support. The quality of a translation is very subjective and always disputed. You and I, we both know the case of Constance Garnett, her legendary works and the further revised editions of the same books by different translators. Dostoyevsky is still translated into English and every translator claims his version to be better than the existing ones.

The most important factor (or maybe the problem) is the emergence and increasing importance of 'Indian Writing in English'. It lessens the urgency to translate. I have many anthologies of world poetry. They don't feature any Hindi poet or poets from other Indian languages. Most of the time, they include a couple of Indian English poets, because they are easily available and accessible. So if readers in the US or the UK want to read literature from India, they will end up reading Salman Rushdie, Amitav Ghosh, Arundhati Roy, Vikram Seth and so on. Whatever India is, in the West it is written by Indian writers writing in English. In the late nineties Salman Rushdie wrote in an article words to the effect that Indian writers working in English have produced stronger literature compared to the other Indian languages.

What were the consequences of Rushdie's article? Indian writers working in English started making more news at the international level. But that didn't help Indian literature. I've read somewhere that in the last five years, more than two thousand books in English translation were published in the US. Only 19 among them were translated from South Asian languages, and among those 19, only 3 were from Indian languages, one each from Hindi, Urdu and Bengali.

Why do Indian writers writing in English have such success in the West? It is not because they 'truly' write India, but because they write an idea of India that the West has itself developed. The whole world including India has convinced itself of the 'fact' that English is the only writing that represents India.

Hindi writers are successful in their own language, but nobody notices it outside their language. Hindi still is the most widely spoken language here. It produces the highest numbers of books each year. Sales of these books are on the increase.

Most Hindi writers either don't know or don't realize the situation I have described. They almost have confined themselves to the mayhem of their ghetto and are quite happy there. It has its own advantages and disadvantages. The advantage is they don't feel any extra pressure and write what they want to write. The disadvantage is their writing, sometimes, lacks an ambitious, competitive, modern edge. I usually describe it in the language of cricket: they play in smaller grounds and hence their sixers are never huge.

In this scenario, the life of a Hindi writer is quite difficult. A Hindi writer's struggle is peculiar. It is quite different from a Polish or Spanish or an Italian writer's struggle. They don't face the plurality of languages. A Hindi writer does. They have the support of history. A Hindi writer doesn't. Their literature is historically accepted worldwide. The literature of my language doesn't even find a proper mention in the history of world literature. Their languages still carry a strong sense of pride. The pride of my language is brutally wounded. They have a legacy of great writers, well known to the world. My language has a legacy of great writers, who are unknown to the world. In the international market, their languages produce a hundred-odd books in English translation each year. My language produces none. It seems the value of my language is very low.

VINOD KUMAR SHUKLA

Translated by Arvind Krishna Mehrotra

Vinod Kumar Shukla was born in 1937 and started writing when he was in his early twenties. A meeting in 1958 with the Marxist Hindi poet Gajanan Madhav Muktibodh, who was teaching Hindi in a local college, was crucial to his development as a poet.

Rajnandgaon (where he was born) and Raipur (where he spent his working life), for Shukla encompass the known world, and in one way or another he has always written about them. In his imagination, the two places merge into one, become one neighbourhood. As he writes in 'Old Veranda,' his autobiographical essay published in n+1 in Spring 2017: 'The old veranda of our house in Rajnandgaon is now in the house in Raipur. The pole star in Raipur is the same pole star that was in Rajnandgaon.' In the poem below, the joint family that 'lived together | under one roof' no longer does, but Shukla wishes it had been otherwise. Does not grass continue to live next to grass? Is there nothing that we can learn from it, from mud, from wind?

Inherent to Shukla's writing is the element of play, with which he leavens his essentially moral temperament. The things he plays with are the most ordinary. It is only after he has finished with the playing do we realize that the play was deadly serious. An example would be his poem 'This year too in these plains', in which he looks at a map of India and asks why mountains, rivers, cities should remain fixed in one place: 'The Himalayas seem unfair | to a place that does not have the Himalayas.' If all places were to be displaced 'and brought near all other places', there would be no displacement, no internal migration 'because of drought, terrorism, or war.'

Had we all lived together...

Had we all lived together
          under one roof
without separate kitchens –
grandfather, great aunt,
father, uncle, siblings –
and remained in
the same neighbourhood.
Grass lives next to grass,
mud next to mud,
and in the wind live
storms, hurricanes,
and scent-laden gusts.
Unbroken, without knots,
the earth's wind is one
with our breathing.

JOY GOSWAMI

Translated by Sampurna Chattarji

Joy Goswami was born in Kolkata on 10 November, 1954. At the age of five his family moved to Ranaghat, a mofussil town in Bengal. The death of his father when he was a child, and his mother when he was twenty-nine, left deep scars – these are losses that haunt many of his poems. He was nineteen when his poems began to be published in magazines, appearing over the next decade in important literary journals, establishing him as 'one of the finest poets in the 'post-Jibanananda Das era' of Bengali poetry' (Arundhathi Subramaniam in *PIW*) who went on to garner both critical and popular acclaim. I began translating his poetry in 2005, drawn to the surreal, intense, allusively mythological universe of *Ashes, Burnt by the Sun* (1999); the pursuit of a language beyond the limits of language in *Shiva, My High* (2005); the unnerving coexistence of the quotidian and the cosmic in *No More Than a Spurt of Time* (2011). Here was a poet interested in the atomic structure of words; in looking at poems as bursts of energy that could annihilate as much as regenerate; who reinvested the poet's role with urgency. If at times the poet's voice seemed to come from another planet – a voice that spoke to darkness, scorpions, constellations, where Death could sit sipping unmentioned substances on your windowsill like an uninvited but not necessarily unwelcome guest – at others, the poet's living tone ran through the world, teasing, cajoling, jibing, splintering every normative utterance. After the publication of Joy Goswami's *Selected Poems* (Harper Perennial, 2014), I turned my attention to his prose poems, where I found a new music; new levels of rage and compassion, awareness and warning. The poems featured here are from his most recent collection, *Whiplash* (Signet Press, 2017).
From *Srigal: Ekadosh* (Jackal: Eleven)

Poet

Morning is the utmost tree. Ocean, the utmost wind. Desert is the
utmost sun. Rain, the utmost invocation. Bird, the utmost prey.
Water, the utmost mind. Earth, the utmost poet. Seeds in earth.
Crops from seeds. Look, there's the rice carousing in the sun! On
cabbage leaves, on spinach leaves, there's the glittering dew. All of this
the earth has written in its own hand. It's the earth that says, sit down
dear, dinner's served.

from *Boddhobhoomi Ekadosh* (*Boddhobhoomi: Eleven*)

2

Every single one of my assumptions about birds is now a dead bird.
Beak open, wings splayed. Right next to it, its own overturned nest.
There was a raging storm that night. As it fell to earth, did it know it
was already dying? That not a single one of my assumptions about
birds will survive, I have only just understood.

3

Try changing your sleep. The kind of sleep that keeps you awake all
night. Try changing your mind. So that not another drop of melody
can enter your ears. The moment a melody enters, these killing fields
will become intolerable. The vultures in the trees will not be able to
accept the ambush of hyenas in the bushes any more. One will want
to call a vulture a vulture. There will be a terrible fracas. Forget the
name: Suman Kalyanpur. Forget it the way you forgot the Gayatri
Mantra. Because that's the name within which the musical mode is

located. That's what kalyan means: the slow blooming of stars in the sky. Careful. They cannot be allowed to bloom. Pick up a fistful of mud from this field. Tamp the bloodstained mud onto the stars, their light needs to be extinguished, immediately.

NOTE: Boddhobhoomi specifically refers to the burial site of those intellectuals (teachers, educationists, journalists, writers, doctors, lawyers) who were killed in December 1971, in what was then East Pakistan; the mass grave was discovered only after the war of liberation and the formation of Bangladesh. Suman Kalyanpur (b.1937) is an Indian singer. The Gayatri Mantra is a sacred Vedic chant to the sun. Kalyan is a mode that qualifies a raga in Indian classical music; the noun also signifies 'well-being'.

AFZAL AHMED SYED

Translated by Taimoor Shahid

The two nazms translated here reflect the wide range of Syed's subject matter and its treatment, while also demonstrating the understated haunting which characterizes his work. Syed's poetry has been shaped partly by his traumatic experiences – that of the 1971 Bangladesh Liberation War, and the 1976 Lebanese Civil War, both of which he witnessed as a young man. The first poem reflects Syed's characteristic treatment of human experience: intimate observation delivered in detached form. While Syed recovers for us the historically peculiar – the name of the slum in Dhaka (Mohakhali Settlement), the character's social class (garment-factory workers, migrant labour), the circumstances of her daily existence (bamboo walls, tin roof, ilish fish, VCRs) and the history of Bangladesh (it has been freed twice) – his poem transcends the immediate and the political by collapsing it into the defiant human will to live a fulfilling life in the face of dispossessions. History, circumstance, poetry, and lived experience come together in his bare, yet penetrating, voice.

In the second poem, Syed establishes himself as the poet's poet, a poet par excellence who can pluck the horse from a mundane election poster in Islamabad and transform it into a poetic exhortation that transcends all contexts. The horse becomes the universal that weds Greek Mythology to the Napoleonic Wars, Pharaonic Egypt to Abrahamic Traditions, and al-Mutanabbi to Giambologna. It's unclear whether the invoked horse – found on a poster in Aabpara, a commercial centre in Pakistan's capital city, often the site of political rallies and protests, and urged to trot Constitution Avenue, a major road that hosts institutions like the Parliament, the Senate, and the Supreme Court – is real, or a metaphor for another majestic quadruped that features prominently in Pakistani politics: a major, and the current ruling party of

Pakistan, famously has a lion as an election symbol. Whatever the case, Syed's claim on the image transcends the temporal and the political by successfully wedding its poetic urgency with the urgency of the form: an earnest plea addressed to The Horse, the poem's rightful audience.

Both the poems here were first published in *Rokoko aur Dusri Dunyaen* (Rococo and Other Worlds, 2000).

A Portrait on Page 163

Sitting beside a foreign river
   she does not need
   to remember her city

She is happy in Mohakhali Settlement
   which is discussed in a lecture
   delivered in Copenhagen

She can even swim
   to the garment factory
   where she began working
   in tenth grade

She watches three consecutive films a week
   on a communal VCR
   and buys a kilo of ilish
   on the first of every month

She does not have an ailing father
   a loafing brother
   or a lurking enemy

It is not that she will remain unmarried
all her life
there is a boy
who teaches in a school
and does not want to be a driver in New York
nor a cook in Karachi

In her house of bamboo walls
and tin roof
she is happy

When she was not selected for a role
in the community theatre
she was not
aggrieved

The same day
she was inducted in a group of girls
to protest before the office
of the Water Supply Board

Nobody taught her how to be happy
she
knows that

She does not know where
the line of poverty
traverses her body

Her poor country
has been freed
twice

She is freer and happier
than the whole world

Upon the Selection of the Horse as the Electoral Symbol for a Political Party

Do not appear on a rotten piece of paper, do not hide Odysseus and his wicked aides inside your body, leave the posters plastered on the walls of Aabpara, and trot down Constitution Avenue neighing, get under the thighs of Amazon women, do not seat Nelson's statue on your back at Trafalgar Square, go straight to the studio of Giambologna, enter without knocking, take al-Mutanabbi to the Sultan's tent, for the first time a poet will present his paean atop a horse, get out of the bank's locker, break the vault, and topple the pillars of the central office like Samson, do not let the lawn mower mow your mane, Eve is buying an apple for Adam from the supermarket, grab it and present it to your favourite mare, ride the boats and discover the America that Isabella couldn't buy for all the jewels in her crown, make Alexander the Great and Julius Caesar your mercenaries, pull the bier of Adonis, discover the sunken ships, hunt for inland treasures, invent a new kind of grass, nail the moon in your hoof, do not look back at Minotaur, Jesus does not have a horse, take him to Mary Magdalene's house on this rainy night, Nefertiti has never seen a horse, she will prostrate herself taking you for God, do not let your back be branded, do not let your picture be stamped.

VIMMI SADARANGANI

Translated by Gopika Jadeja

Vimmi Sadarangani is a Sindhi poet from India. Her family migrated to the region of Kutch in India during the partition, like many Sindhi Hindu families. While Sindhi is an official language in India (it was included in the Eighth Schedule of the Indian Constitution through an amendment in 1966), it is a language in exile. The many Sindhi schools that were established by the refugee Sindhis have been closed and the number of young Sindhis in India who are literate and fluent in Sindhi has been dwindling. Many Indians view Sindhi language and culture as alien. In Gujarat, where many Sindhi Hindus went as refugees, they are viewed as different and have been made to feel unwelcome. Much of this is due to the heterogeneous nature of Hinduism in Sind, where it embraces elements of Islam and Sikhism.

Nostalgia for her Sind, which she has heard of in her grandmother's stories and visits only as an adult, is a strain that runs through Vimmi's poetry, as in the poem 'History'. In 'History' she builds on memory and history and the tension between the history she has heard from her grandmother and attempts of archaeologists to dig 'the city of stones | to make history bear witness'. The Dancing Girl and seals are artefacts found from the Indus Valley at the site of Mohenjo-daro in Sind. Besides her identity as Sindhi, Vimmi's poems also explore her identity as a woman. In 'I do not know anything about myself' she explores her body, which is part of the natural world. She names her parts and yet this naming of parts cannot grasp the essence, there is something that eludes knowledge.

I do not know anything about myself

Birds
my tongue.

Winds
my breath.

Sky
my head.

Clouds
my clothes.

Sun
my body.

River
my heart.

Yet, something seems amiss
If you find out, let me know
for I know nothing about myself.

History

It was probably
at the age of fourteen
that I heard
about a city of stones and broken walls.

They say this is the place our ancestors
called home

My grandmother used to tell me stories
of that city
that her grandmother told her

The court dancer had been cursed
One of her arms became longer
than the other arm
It is said she had committed a crime

She tried to
battle the termites in the palace
with her bare hands

There used to be great baths in the city
No one knows how
but one day it all drowned

Toys
Seals
Dancing girl
Alive
Dead
All buried
in the sands

I hear that
archaeologists are digging at
the city of stones
to make history bear witness.

'Heer Ranjha' is a classic Punjabi rural poem about doomed lovers. I've
incorporated elements of this story along with the classic Persian poem
'Layla and Majnun' which is similarly about a doomed relationship. Both
stories explore complex ideas about love, about community, and about
spiritual ideals. Both stories have been rewritten by many writers over
the past centuries. In my rendition, I explore the possibility of merging
the two stories to create a fresh narrative. I have read several translations
of each long poem to help me create my own unique translation. The
excerpt published here is from an earlier part of my poem.

Backlashing Baglash & Jaglash

With a gnash rolling-pin in hand
at the entrance to the family courtyard,
and facing Majnoo as he returned home,
was his eldest sister-in-law, Baglash.

Baglash prodded her bony-voice at Majnoo,
'Surely surely it is but weeks since your father died.
A father butting death with grief for his wife's death.
A father who is surely surely not plying the new harvest
now his marital oaths are drowned.

Why is it you are outstaying your oats?
You are a curse upon your father's dotage.
No farming rags, no mansome tool in hand
instead you are drowning
books and tunes by day then at night you are skimming
the moon in your bright clothes of a bride!'

Majnoo was all whimsy,
'I skim in bright clothes to mirror the dream
of my true love.'

Baglash was hard and dreamless; was stinked as manure;
was in Majnoo's face and not going dry,
'How many men have perish-to-perished
trying to catch even a snip of the famed queen
who was locked behind walls, moats and guards:
the great Rani Kokilan...Go catch your own rani.
Why are you crapping sharam upon us
        by mucking with a cowpat girl?'

Standing at the border of Majnoo's bedroom,
        also with rolling-pin in hand
        and slapping it in the other hand loudly,
was Jaglash, the twin sister of Baglash.

They were hill girls wedded to men from the plains.
They wielded stunning erect noses; moistless enormous blank eyes,
and power-plaits – long and black-hard as a pestle.
They'd churned their natures on the dense airs of the heights
and the grip-heat of the plains.
Instead of a temperate clime,
        what came up through their moods were ramrod projectile knuckles.

Jaglash was married to the second eldest brother of Majnoo.
Jaglash wore an eye-patch after a fight with a bull.
Jaglash swung her bulk-thigh across Majnoo's door
to block it from shutting. And said,

'Girls at the spinning wheel
between sucking up the thread
say now your head is out of books
your mouth is frisking with a flute. Mucky boy!'

Majnoo called back, 'Out of my way, eye-patch.
For spilling Roslinder's milk – I have paid humbly.'

'Are we wanting humbling by a cowpat girl?' said Baglash
who had moved behind Majnoo. Jaglash laughed; her own laugh –
she spiked it – quick-stunted it – said,
'The peacock is too much cocky-flapping.
Let the tiger be a glint of claws!'

Baglash and Jaglash hoisted up their large rolling pins
then, from behind and ahead,
threw them down for Majnoo's skull.

Majnoo moved fast after feeling a blow
smoke one of his shoulders.
He heard Jaglash let out a high soaring grackle.

The sisters now headed for his head.

They chased him about the courtyard
but Majnoo, with bare time to think,
gave a dozen lively contrariwise dinkings.
He then slipped low, then jumped outerbound
with great speed
as the wood weapons swung throoping for his skull.

Eventually, Majnoo pushed Jaglash out of the way
and was inside and bolting his door.
Now nursing his bruised shoulder.

The sound of the bolt retched on the throats
of the twins.
All they could do with their expletives
was to snot the brass door knob.

MONIKA KUMAR

Translated by Sampurna Chattarji

Monika Kumar is a young poet who writes in Hindi. Born in 1977 in Nakodar (a small town in Punjab's Jalandhar district), she is based in Chandigarh, where she teaches English Literature. The poems in this selection are symptomatic of her desire to record the world while retreating from it. It is this attention to the momentary – the urge to understand and inscribe, not in order to simplify the 'mystique or incomprehensibility of the moment', not even to resolve it, but to be in a conscious state of receptivity, even grace – that animates Monika's poems. She has spoken to me of being 'greatly enchanted by seeing people creating interesting things with simple and seemingly insignificant materials, like a mason building a wall, a tailor sewing and hemming with such precision, a carpenter making window-frames from an impossible log of wood; and mother kneading flour or chopping a watermelon. They all brought a magnitude to the things they worked with, making them intelligible, comprehensive and beautiful.' This is what I feel Monika does with the words she works with, making intelligible, comprehensive, beautiful things out of the phenomena she observes. Tonally, her poems inhabit a direct, conversational register. There is a lucid transparency to the lines. She is not interested in flamboyant gestures. It is the stillness of her gaze and the profound necessity of her questions that earn my admiration. I had the pleasure of meeting her in Chandigarh at a translation workshop organized by Literature Across Frontiers (LAF) in November 2016. Hearing Monika read her poems in the original (and seeing how beautifully they travelled into languages such as Slovenian, Galician and Maltese from bridge translations) made me want to work, in collaboration with her, on fresh English versions, which are featured here for the first time.

On Seeing a Watermelon

Seeing a watermelon
was my introduction to vastness.

I can only approximate
how much I love you:

by the handful,
as much as the sea
or not at all.

Approximations fail me
when I look at a watermelon.
How red it will be
how fleshy
how its meditative eyes would be arrayed inside.

You were stubborn in your insistence:
the earth is round as an orange.
You refused to accept
it could also be like a watermelon.

Anyway!
I lied to you
when I said I can tell you, approximately,
how much I love you.

All estimations are a failure of my language.
I need a few signs of exclamation
mad transports
that will gently translate my failures.

The Dangers of Hindsight

For a moment, forget hindsight
prudence and reconsideration.
Burdened by history and experience
you will render even me speechless with your reasoning.
What emerges from hindsight are sieved and scrubbed words.
But what I want from you
is an answer
artless
sudden
oblivious of history
refuting experience.
That's when you give me an undivided yes
or a simple no, meaning no.
Otherwise all you give me are references
to all those experiences
I wasn't even part of.

To make any sense of history
I need your
sudden response.
In its freshness
I can see better

the peanuts hidden in their sturdy shells
the fresh oil full in their ripened seeds.

Window Seat

To be happy in life one needs very little.
That 'little' can sometimes be no more than this:
when we are all set to travel by bus or train or plane
we should be lucky enough
to get a window seat.
And, having bought a ticket,
avoided arguments with co-passengers,
stowed away our luggage safely,
after all of this,
we should be lucky enough to slip easily into ourselves.

Between home and the wild how hard to find such places
where we can take naps light as flowers,
have hundreds of trees cradle our sleep
or the whiteness of clouds carry us towards nothingness.
To wake from this small sleep is a miracle,
this sleep repairs our dwindling being,
restores us to our position,
brings us back to the question
of who we are,
which we ask ourselves once again,
even if our only answer
is to burst into tears.

LEELADHAR JAGOORI

Translated by Sarabjeet Garcha

Inspired by the folk songs of Garhwal, Leeladhar Jagoori (born 1940) wrote his earliest poems in his mother tongue, Garhwali. He fled from home at the age of twelve, only to return eleven years later, soon after which he was recruited as a soldier in the Garhwal Rifles. What had begun as an extensive love of Hindi literature in his teens culminated into a full-blown passion for writing by the time he was in his early twenties, and he realised before long that he wasn't cut out for the army. On an impulse, he dispatched a letter (with unpaid postage!) to the then defence minister of India, V. K. Krishna Menon, expressing his desire to quit the army. To his utter surprise and relief, the wish was gracefully granted, and thus Hindi poetry found one of its most prolific practitioners.

Jagoori believes that 'poetry teaches prose to perceive the value of words and also imparts to language the power to create words consonant with experience. Even in bad and uninteresting times, poetry preserves the lively interest in being human' (*Eeshvar Ki Adhyakshata Mein* (Under God's Supervision)). His own interest in the world – even in the most wearisome version of it that is teeming with countless objects – is nothing short of sprightly and wondrous, and he transports readers to a wonderland that can compress 'millions of years in one day' with his brilliant imagery, supple language and masterly diction. The range of subjects he chooses for his poetry is astonishingly wide, but he is equally adept at concentrating on a single object and coming up with multiple poetic responses to it. For instance, he has just finished writing a series of poems on the theme of stone. Despite his incredible fecundity, he never approaches one city by the same road. And that is also the definitive way to approach his poetry, which delights, surprises, amuses, ruffles, comforts, pierces, touches, elevates and, ultimately, satiates.

The Muntjac

The muntjac has been calling since evening
the tiger and the cremation ground are shining in the moonlight
in the ghostly shadow of the trees
the rocks have reached some other world
the summits appear soft as a bull's hump

the muntjac has been calling since evening as if separated
in this reality the tiger comes out of the bushes
to hunt in the moonlight where the muntjac has been calling
since evening as if wanting to tell about its fear to the whole forest

Grandmother says it'll rain tomorrow the poor
muntjac has been calling since evening
rain in winter means snowfall directly
and that the wild animals will come to the hamlet

in the moonlight Grandmother helps her grandson to piss
make it fast or the tiger will come for you
the child hears the school bell
here rolls the tumbler of water

children who came back from the school beyond
the mountain have gone to sleep inside without covering themselves
outside there's moonlight and the muntjac goes running
leaving a scent

the tiger is waiting for it near the hedge
where the water first rises
below the bushes and the rocks

and in which the abundant moon is visible
the muntjac comes running from all the four directions
and the tiger is waiting for it on a spot
near the water
and the grass is shining near where
the murder will take place in the moonlight
the grass is shining near the tiger stripes

suddenly the tiger sees that the muntjac is sitting on the moon
and that several tigers turned into stones are sitting
at the riverbank

waiting enervates everyone that is hungry
the tired tiger dozes off
the forest takes its midnight breath
dreams enter homes
the moon says to the first-grade student
I have saved this shadow of the muntjac for you
you must save the muntjac yourself
learn to identify its favourite
delicious grass and nutritious leaves

like an enterprise of vegetation
the river is shining in the moonlight
on the bank sits the tiger turned stony in sleep
the earth is moistening
the darkness is dwindling

towards the soft peak of the western mountain
away from the yawn of the hungry tiger

nibbling at the jewelled sky
a mud-coloured muntjac is descending
the trees are getting over the nocturnal shadow

I See Myself ...

I see myself
always loaded with a knapsack
I see myself
always running

some horses die midway
some trains penetrate the ocean
some aeroplanes
crash into the horizon and disappear
and more and more blood
turns into water

even then I see myself
always running
and see that the earth
weighs upon my back like a knapsack

ANITHA THAMPI

Translated by J. Devika

It is my firm belief that the poem would have been impossible to translate out of Malayalam if one were not closely familiar with the visual landscape and the intimate quality of nature that it meditates on. The water of the region is indeed reddish brown and reeks of iron. If one had not directly experienced it, perhaps one's translation would have been helplessly literal and powerless to capture its rhetorical glimmer. Also, it would be impossible to plumb the depths of this poem if one were not familiar with the history of the tragedy of politics here. Without such knowledge, the translator cannot really distinguish the layers of meaning that the poem nurtures. And finally, if one did not know of the cultural politics of Kerala in which the northern waters of the Nila stand for elite traditional culture and the murky waters of Alappuzha, for radical non-elite cultural upheaval, the translation would have certainly missed the poem's subtle meditation on this politics and the poet's own implication in it. Alappuzha is a small town in Kerala with a globally connected but very specific story of its own. It even had a unique visual tapestry, much of which is intact despite the brutal assault of first-world-worshipping consumerism. It has a place in the modern history of this unique region in India: Kerala. It has witnessed momentous events in the cultural history of Kerala, and its unique idiom was the bearer of the literature of social change in the middle decades of the twentieth century, which altered the social and political fabric of society here like nowhere else in India. It is also, today, a melancholic place, of decline and devastation – of politics, ideals, nature. Anitha's poem captures all of this with exquisite economy. Like a diamond set brilliantly, the many shades and lights of the town glint through those words.

This poem ('Alappuzha *Vellam*') is being joint-published in India by
The Indian Quarterly (http://indianquarterly.com) and in the UK
by *Modern Poetry in Translation*

Alappuzha *Vellam*

She, of Alappuzha.
She, of that soil's charcoal-tints.

When she writes in poetry,
she writes, *jalam!*

Attoor the Poet asked:
It's *vellam*, isn't it?
She, of Alappuzha,
the girl with palm-thatch braids;
daughter of the muddy water,
rotting-coconut-husk-reeking water,
faintly-briny-tasting water,
bright-tea-burnished water.

For her, *jalam*
means the clear liquid
that reigns
in Wayanad, *Nila*-land,
hill-land, southern-land.
That which falls off the sky
and is un-fallen on the earth,
that which has no smell,

the gift of the deep,
colourless water which beholds
far distances, towering heights,
Water that does not wilt and lie still
in the plains.

It holds the gods,
charming temples,
daily worship, divine feasts,
year after year, festive flags,
trunk-waving tuskers,
the brimming crowd.

Alappuzha's fine soil
gets the monthlies.
Thus is born, *vellam*.
It stains,
it washes, it bathes,
it stretches out in pain,
it gets up, walks,
it stays sleepless,
touching not its mate-water.
Untamed and sharp-tongued,
couldn't care less
for clarity.
Fitful are its depths.

Their-Selves are their Deities.
Sacrifice lies sprawled on
its stones, all over inner worlds and out.
Oars, wheels, coir-spinning *ratts*.

The songs of the shattered throat.
Headless flagpoles.
The nod of the yellowed
palm-frond ears.

The monsoon that dances
all agog, like the beach at fish-thronging *chaakara*,
pitiless summer, spitting fire
as the white sand scorches, sears.
Vellam keeps step, it brims, it sinks.
Bowls and pans,
storing pots full,
fish-scaly skin that clings
stubbornly to them – the *vellam*'s pain.

Canals, boat-jetty,
Stone Bridge and Iron Bridge,
pond, backwater, rolling water-weed carpets,
hyacinth-bloom-smiles,
the glow of coconut fibre-gold,
the tang of dissolved iron,
the sodden scent of sweat,
all in the waters of Alappuzha.
It wobbles, it dims,
dissolves in the distance,
melts into images
the birds alone see.

Decades have passed
and she's homed in southern waters.
Yet while writing,

delving the depths of memory
she, of Alappuzha's hues
she, of Alappuzha's hair
still knows not: *jalam*, or *vellam*?
She turns, she knows
but she turns not, she knows not.

The throat stays parched.

NOTE: *chaakara* is a unique coastal phenomenon in which fish
congregate in large numbers due to the formation of mud banks
during the summer monsoon

I was born in Calcutta and spent the first five years of my life there. This city, which was once the second city of the British Empire, was where English literature was first introduced as a discipline of study, to civilise the natives.

I spent the next eight years in Bombay, and returned to the city of my birth for another five before moving to the USA on my own when I was eighteen. After seven years in America, I moved to London in 2005 on a British government scholarship. I have lived in London ever since.

My writing grows out of this fractured upbringing across three continents. The linguistic effects of this fracturing are peculiar. I grew up with three languages (English, Bengali, and Hindi) and started learning another (French) when I was fourteen. Strangely, given the formative years of my schooling took place in Bombay, I cannot read what is – ostensibly – my mother tongue (Bengali), though I still speak it. I am illiterate in the language of my ancestors.

'Elegy, Father's City' emerges from this illiteracy. I spent my adolescent years flâneur-ing through the streets of Calcutta. Yet, I am forever severed from it as I read the great literature of the city, in translation. This long poem is my attempt at translating the city back to myself, in English, the language that still colonises the modern Indian state, and mind. This translation, the poem, is filled with fragments, a sense of the incomplete, little alleyways of thought and image, half-spoken utterances. It is also a poem of mourning, and in that sense, it is haunted by ghosts, like Calcutta itself, and fed by the ghosts of words I can't read, but only see as strange hieroglyphs, borne across, translated, from a broken, voiceless past.

Elegy, Father's City

'Something undreamt of was lurking everywhere [in Calcutta], and
every day the uppermost question was: where, oh where would I come
across it?'
– Rabindranath Tagore

Dear Baba,

the axe of your death lodged in my skull, I
walk Calcutta.

(the second city of a
burning empire)

I am a poor fakir, made
mad by a comedy that instant
news feeds can't convey.

Your body I carry, a one-string instrument, in my
sweating hands.

I have lost my voice.
When I open my mouth, flies

drop into the city's sewers.

♦

Park Street, singularity.

Bloodstains of Christmas – a large bunny Santa Claus, glowing
starfish stretched across the width of the street, green dripping
lights –

are still there.

I spent my youth drinking in the
bars of this angular thoroughfare.

I scan them
(your eyeballs mashed in my head),
the old ones that have been
around since the days of the American GIs.

Jazzy Trincas, Kwalitys, the legend called Olympia where the
waiters know me like their own children.

Imitations like Moulin Rouge
stare down the new clientele with
timbered, glazed glass.

Flashy bars have come up,
swanky temples for exotic cars.

Magazines and books litter the sidewalk.
Shoppers in jeans hop over the crutches of a beggar,
his hair wired and messy, his
clothes a tattered brown.

Park Hotel leaks caterpillar cars.

The crowds hustle. The yellow Ambassador cabs
crank up the volume.

◆

I turn to Free School street.
New restaurants – Chinese, European – have
opened.

The road is patchy. The sidewalks are narrow and broken.
A Muslim beggar (all the beggars are Muslim), eyes
blackened and bandaged, is

led by a child in rags.

('Is man no more than this,' I hear you say,
bard-voiced, slicked in the raging,

boiling
howl of the city)

He is old and carries a long bamboo stick.
He sings in Sufi. As he and his child shift
pass me, the
smell of him
stays like

black fume.

◆

I see more of what I've seen before.

Masjids, ramshackle multi-cuisine hotels, the old
Armenian school where Thackeray was

born, where I played cricket.

Tiny side-streets with internet cafes,
down-and-out cinemas,
edge my sight and vision.

This long, snaking, potholed
street is a noisy bedlam,

bandaged, infernoed.

(Empty hand-pulled rickshaws are
lit triangles)

❖

Chinese leather shoe stalls, the
old chimney-soup-dive,

still there.

Flea-racks selling ancient gramophones and
botched vinyl
line the pavement.

A clutch of Europeans
jive to Laila o Laila. Next to them, a Bengali
dressed in a dhoti flips through Bach's concertos.

◆

The gunpowder evening crackles –

burning onions on a steel tray.

The dope-heads and urchins sleep, float above the city in
black n' white dreams.

A fire engine roils by.

I slip into Sudder Street, noticing new hotels and
Thai spas, festering like unwanted cysts.

Hotel Fairlawn is still there, green as
Marvell's thoughts in a garden. (A sanctuary for noisy exotic
birds called tourists)

The hashed backpackers still
louche about in blue-sky cafe,

swallowing pancakes.

Concrete street-scabs are lined with
broken water pipes. Dhobis
iron clothes on wood and stone.

Scrappy joints advertise chowmein and momos.
A flute-seller, a manicured peacock,
plays a tune, his sound like a sax.

◆

This is where Tagore had his vision, you whisper,
suddenly, from the other side, voice
ruffled in the darkening of the evening.

My laughter is the taste of blood. I
choke on it.

I turn, head towards New Market,
down a little street whose name I've forgotten.

A squawk of communist flags greets me.
A drift from the city's past.

These flags are riot wings. I

exhale.

◆

A divine amputee, legs chopped, bandaged arms,
rolls himself up and down, repeating

'Allah Allah', his voice
big as a bullfight.

All around him are people dressed for the
mania of buying and selling.

Stores with bladerunner gadgets.
Tacky malls, bridal boutiques.

The reflections on the glass of a leather store are
television.

This vein of a street is littered with
cracked tea-urns made of earth.

And plates of leaves
stitched with the remains of
chickpeas, bread, puffed rice. The

sting of tamarind
pulls out my eyes.

◆

A friend I haven't seen in years is there,
waiting for me.

It could have been you,
in your youth.

A stylish cat from a
black and white film.

He wears a blue blazer, an electric dhoti,
starched white shirt, a jewelled walking stick. He

drinks from a pitcher of water. He
wipes his mouth. He

puts an arm around my broken shoulder.

He takes your charred, blackened body from me.

When he does, your body
melts to ash.

Clouds scatter, darken,

scatter.

◆

I am young,
again,

drunk on these same streets, with
old friends.

You are not dead, dear father.
You have gone away, on holiday,

somewhere

An Indivisible Mind

New *Selected Poems* by Shuntarō Tanikawa, translated by
William I. Elliott and Kazuo Kawamura, Carcanet Press, 2015

Born in 1931 in Tokyo to well-regarded intellectual and artistic
parents, Shuntarō Tanikawa is a veteran in the post-war/
contemporary Japanese poetry scene. He has published some sixty
collections of poetry and several books of essays and non-fiction, as
well as plays, music, and diverse cross-genres of media and print. As
a national award-winning translator, he is known in Japan for his
popular renderings of *Peanuts* and *Mother Goose* nursery rhymes. The
influence of translation and other artistic practices – music and the
visual arts, among others – is evident in his poems, as seen in the
piece '10. (in the manner of Charlie Brown)' from the sequence 'At
Midnight in the Kitchen I Just Wanted to Talk to You', which he
concludes with idiosyncrasy: 'It's not easy to change the subject.' In
short, he is one of the rare poets in Asia, and worldwide, whose
oeuvre can be defined as cross-disciplinary and all-encompassing.

Tanikawa started composing poems when he was only a teenager.
He published his debut collection *Two Billion Light-Years of Solitude* in
1952. Given the longevity of his poetic success and the prodigious
and ongoing output, the task of adequately representing his work in
a two-hundred-page volume of *Selected Poems* would seem an
impossible one. Any effort to do so is bound to shortchange readers
of Tanikawa's writings which span sixty years, compounded with the
fact that this Japanese master's poems are translations in a non-
Asian language of entirely disparate linguistic constructs, history,
and thought. For this and other reasons, I find much to applaud in
co-translators William I. Elliott's and Kazuo Kawamura's recent
publication of his *New Selected Poems*, not least their bravery and

longstanding faith in the poet's voice, vision, and innovative aesthetics. Elliott and Kawamura introduce the volume with a brief essay 'Timeless Tanikawa', which is followed by four to ten poems from each of the chosen twenty-two Tanikawa collections. Presented in a chronological order, the poems are mostly brief and free verse, the latter considered a refreshing departure from traditional Japanese poetics. Readers, however, can still get a feel of Tanikawa's prose from a dozen or more prose poems that his co-translators have culled from the two volumes, *Definitions* (1975) and *Coca-Cola Lessons* (1980). Because of this broad sampling, there isn't a specific thematic round-up or structure throughout the book, and I found the introductory essay somewhat too brief for the weight of such a literary corpus. But these editorial difficulties should not be viewed as failings: for more than four decades, Elliott and Kawamura have been working on Tanikawa and have published numerous book-length translations, so readers should feel encouraged to seek these books out if they wish to enjoy more coherence in terms of specific collections.

Tanikawa Shuntarō's poems aren't difficult to read. On the contrary, they are usually accessible and communicative. That his poems, often described as bestselling, would appeal to both serious poetry lovers and mainstream readers, doesn't strike me as a surprise. Critics, in fact, might find Tanikawa's accessibility a flaw, since the distinct conversational quality of his poems can also undercut their lyric force and density. A couple of them come across as informal or 'easily written', and so diluted and more 'spoken word' than page poetry:

> I have to go now
> right now
> but don't know where.
> [...]

Have to go by myself
but don't know why
I'm sorry, Mum.
Treat Dad nice.
[...]
I have to go now.

From 'Goodbye', *Naked* (1988)

I'm going to write you a postcard.
I'll say that I'm fine;
but that's not really true.
I mean, I'm not sick, either.

From '7', *At Midnight in the Kitchen I Just Wanted to
Talk to You* (1975)

But in several instances the performative aspect is felt even on
the page and Tanikawa Shuntarō appears in control of lyrical
tautness and intensity. This has much to do with the philosophical
bent of these poems, in which the poet constantly questions the
existential value of his art and vocation. For example, in one of the
entries ('2 August') for his 'Kita-Karuizawa Diary' he writes:

Every poet kept to his own style until he died.
Style is predestined.

Yet those various styles tempt me –
one, two, three, four...

All styles fascinate me
and I soon grow bored by any one,
just like Don Juan.

Faithful to a woman,
unfaithful to poetry?

But hasn't poetry from the very beginning
been unfaithful to people?

Such dark humour and self-deprecation are characteristic of
Tanikawa Shuntarō, who knows how to talk dirty without being
vulgar, and be cheeky without being insulting. In another entry
('3 August'), he compares poetry and prose metaphorically, and
demonstrates his trademark audacity in the choice of metaphor:

If prose is taken as a rose,
poetry is its fragrance.
If prose is taken as a garbage dump,
poetry is its stench.

I think of Szymborska when reading Tanikawa: uninvolved with
the elusive and narcissistic self, both deal with the contradictions of
our mortal existence by transforming the poetic 'I' into a mirror that
reflects its own beauty and awkwardness – not for the sake of
persuasion, but as a ritual of deconstructing illusions. In 'The Pure
Land' Tanikawa muses, 'I can't escape what I am. | I have readily
exposed my common features to people, | two eyes, two ears, a nose
and a mouth, | maybe because I have something else to hide.'
Compared to Szymborska, Tanikawa appears to use punctuation
more freely, and embrace the grotesque or the absurd more readily.

Confessing that he is 'not interested in titles' because 'making titles is snobbish', he believes that '[t]he mind is indivisible' (from 'At Midnight in the Kitchen I Just Wanted to Talk to You: 9'). And it is his boldness to write about absurdity – or even the ridiculous or trivial nature of writing – without any need to define it that makes his poetry such a rewarding and enduring read:

> In a world of metal and conferences
> a typewriter is typing a typist.
> Law sculpts a black torso
> and bank notes grow rich and buy slaves.
> Therefore
> people can't help longing for wolves.
>
> We mass-produce a million cliffs a minute.
> Next we must experiment making space and time.
>
> This drink is a fairy tale.
> This cracker is a meadow the colour of wheat.
> That cloud is an old-fashioned fugue.
> Anyhow I will make the afternoon snack a fantasy.

From 'A Contemporary Afternoon Snack', *Two Billion Light-Years of Solitude* (1952)

Fiona Sze-Lorrain

A Good European

A *Public Woman, New and Selected Poems* by Benno Barnard,
translated by David Colmer, Eyewear Publishing, 2015

Anglophone readers should rejoice for it has come to pass that the
poetry of one of Europe's key contemporary writers, Benno Barnard, is
now available in these intuitively translated versions from the Dutch
by the Australian David Colmer. One can only speculate as to the
challenge it must have been for Colmer to maintain a grip on Barnard's
highly charged, redoubtably visual narrative poetry, which roams with
expressive intent across the overlapping domains of personal desire
and loss, the essentiality of free thought, outrage at the resilience of
human folly and a certain noble resignation, all coalescing in the
backdraft of historical precedents. But Colmer is still standing resolute
at the end of this imaginatively orgiastic pageant of truth-seeking
swashbuckling lyricism.

This *Selected* is as the title announces, dominated by what is rather
mischievously academically described as ' a verse play in three acts'.
Here Coco, an actress on her beam end, delivers a bravura biographical
performance, by following the tramlines of a life treading the boards,
until that existentially bristling moment when she states 'I am a
woman about to make her debut in the theatre of old age'. Seasoned
with judiciously harvested quotes from Eliot, Chekhov and
Shakespeare, the pages slowly raise and tip a gravel load of self-
flagellation, doubt and poignant self-realization in a rush of tragedy
influenced human insight.

The poems here reflect Barnard's ardent cosmopolitanism and
decisively European pedigree. Barnard, a committed anglophile who
has just set down roots in rural Sussex, is essentially a man of the
north, of 'le plat pays' of Jacques Brel, his natural territory also being

Flanders and its surroundings, where the rich vein of historicity and that curiously 'intercultural' life blood can be tapped. Barnard denies himself a native root, not for reasons of eccentricity, but because he doesn't really know. Is he Dutch, is he Belgian, is he an Englishman posing as a Dutchman or a Flamand? In the end he is a European, a good European, a purveyor of free movement and speech, a modern espousing the humanistic tradition. Staunch defender of openness and declaration, Barnard is nauseated by the orthodox, the fundamentalist, the imperialist, the dread men of scroll-drawn conviction. In Barnard's universe, fluidity, spontaneity, the unexpected, insight through experiment and reactionary boundary breaching are all, but only when harnessed to the gilded chariot of the creative spirit.

The poems here also show intimate warmth, the poignancy of the brief stolen moment, as in the wonderful opener, 'A Kiss in Brussels', which sets the bar high. Note how Colmer has achieved a certain re-assuring rhythm within the wintry sparseness:

> We stand here freezing in our winter coats,
> a kiss prevents my breath from showing white,
> my hand slows to a halt in mid caress,
> I want to let you go, but not tonight –
> my fingers in your hair, the evidence.
> Here for a second in this city park,
> we're two cold lovers mouthing March,
> who kiss as though exchanging quotes.

Barnard's Brussels kiss is personal and private but it also launches the collection by publicly inviting the reader to celebrate the priceless value of a simple act of human intimacy in a world which otherwise appears to have gone insane. In the poem 'Old

Friend', the first lines are like a red triangle road sign stating 'Genuine poet at work':

> The wolves have lain down at your feet
> Your kids have started thinking of kids
> acceptance descends on you like gentle rain.

The towns of Flanders that Barnard has explored over a lifetime pervade the poems and even when not explicitly mentioned, they ghost there and act as a painted backdrop to the theatrical stage where the narrative plays out. In 'Friends' the fair held annually in the south district of Antwerp is alluded to:

> Further further south a Ferris wheel scooped up
> men and women stuffed with chips fear and fertility:
> the fair had laid anchor on its annual quay
> and Antwerp thrilled to a schmaltzy pulse.

The image of lives being 'scooped up' by the Ferris wheel occurs more than once in this collection, for perhaps it is the cyclical mechanism, the industry of the mill-like wheel, which fascinates Barnard, as the human is suddenly lifted as it were from the earth, like some willing mineral, ascending momentarily to elsewhere, only to be brought back down and deposited where they began.

Belgium is core to Barnard's European spiritual enclosure. 'You're good company in this Belgian town', 'We sit here in Belgium explaining our lives...' The poems are peppered with references, even the infamous SS prison so memorably delineated by W G Sebald in his novel Austerlitz wanders into a poem like some sinister interloper and for a reason undeclared we learn from the notes that Brabosch is the Jewish name for Antwerp. Barnard unearths the ambiguities, absurdities and ramifications of life in a dual language nation, recognizing the ensuing cultural labyrinth as confusing tragicomedy, but also as an opportunity for unforeseen and often overlooked (especially by natives of both factions) creative dividends. In the poem 'Ashkenazic' Barnard muses 'For fifty years you've been foreign everywhere' and a little later dreams of 'A room with a view of all the streets of Europe.' Banality is the supreme foe which Barnard strives to outmanoeuvre:

> It is not nothingness
> that terrifies
> but its revelation in banality.

In this collection we are treated to its antithesis, how to be creatively and humanely progressive now 'in these dark times', with the unknown legacy of the European bone yard pulling us up sharp from any satisfying conclusion. Barnard's poems form a rare repository for authenticity in a poetry world overladen with the baggage of parochialism and the 'many too many'. I urge the Anglophone reader with a European bent to explore his work and witness how through the symbiosis of gestated experience and unbiased reflection the shadow of diminishing hope can be at least alleviated if not entirely lifted.

Will Stone

In the Middle of the Fire

Guarding the Air: Selected Poems of Gunnar Harding, translated by Roger Greenwald, Black Widow, 2014

Guarding the Air, winner of the Harold Morton Landon Translation Award of the Academy of American Poets, is ample indeed: beside Roger Greenwald's brief introduction, it offers at the outset Gunnar Harding's refreshingly unpretentious introductions to several of his books, at the end a helpful collection of notes, and in between, 237 pages of poems written over some thirty-five years, in Greenwald's transparent, thoroughly readable translations.

The earliest poems, from *Flowers for James Dean*, 1969, are full of American referents: the pop culture of movies, comic books and Coca-Cola that flooded Sweden after the war, and above all, jazz, the first art form at which Harding tried his hand, followed by painting, and then poetry. Harding arrived in September 1968 in Iowa City for a year at the International Writers' Workshop, while Anselm Hollo was teaching there. The newest American influence, filtered through Hollo's cosmopolitan sensibility, was the poetry of the New York School. The opening stanza of 'The Train in the Background Is the Rock Island Line' captures the tone:

> St. Anselm Hollo crosses the Iowa River
> on horseback. the grass is green
> his head among the clouds.   singing
> no   laughing bing bong bong   it was
> the bells from the white city hall
> with the gilded roof and the two flags
> in Iowa City.

In this instance the playfulness is close to that of Kenneth Koch; there is a blurb from Koch on the back cover of *Guarding the Air*. The year being 1968, the early poems are burdened with political realities: Vietnam, the demonstrations at the Democratic convention in Chicago, the assassinations. A poem taking off from the Errol Flynn movie *Captain Blood*, thrilling to Harding in his youth, is dedicated to Che Guevara; it imagines the Captain sailing into present-day Miami, and ends this way:

> hello gringos. "green grow
> the hills" you sang when you marched
> across the border with your pockets full of
> greenbacks. the ocean is red. it's
> the sunrise. someone has put a burning
> cigar in the bottom corner of the star-spangled banner
> it's morning. the stars grow pale
> one by one

The obvious New York influence disappears early from *Guarding the Air* as Harding's more characteristic imagistic and associative methods go on evolving. Reading on, one is struck by the great range of Harding's interests. One thread consists of historical subjects like the arrival of the Black Death in Sweden, the polar expeditions of Fridtjof Nansen, the exploits of a famous Swedish criminal called Lasse-Maja, the palace of King Minos, the lives of William Blake and, in an entire suite of poems, Dante Gabriel Rossetti. Throughout, there are poems driven by Harding's lifelong interest in his first two arts: jazz and painting. But Harding's own life is never far away. The ten-page 'History Painting' revolves around the life of his Uncle Arthur, living out his life in a mental institution after the woman he loves is denied permission to marry him because he is a lowly blacksmith. One of the most moving of these is the three-part 'Walk through Autumn's Beauty', his elegy for his mother, Karen Harding, perhaps begun before she dies 'because these days grief arrives most often before death, | wearing whatever's available for the occasion'. A middle section fills out the waiting for the end, taking in and making use of even an unlikely, random event:

> You die in me on the train to Gothenburg, where a manic girl
>   comes over to me in the restaurant car and quotes Rilke: "to
>   be no-one's sleep under so many lids"
> and then shouts, "There's a bunch of cows standing there
>   shitting!" in pastures where the birches have only few yellow
> leaves amid the green rushing of eyelids, which droop shut,
> droop shut over No-one's sleep.

The final section is painfully simple:

> I sit on the chair by the bedside.
> Just you and me in the room.
> Almost imperceptibly,
> just me in the room.

The book closes with thirty poems from *The Burning Child*, 2003, in which Harding looks back over his life. Many titles simply name the years they return to, including 1940, the year of his birth. At the centre is the title poem; the note informing us that the town where he was born, like many Swedish towns full of wooden houses, burned down around the turn of the century helps to explain why a young boy might have an exaggerated fear of fire. The poem opens this way:

> It isn't fire that consumes. It's
> fear of the flare-up, especially the nighttime one

in which the past's humiliations won't reveal themselves
and therefore can't be burned up ...
The irreducible element that does not burn is guilt ...

There's no fire, we learn, outside the boy's mind. At the end he
and the poet merge:

But the fear is still there. Fear of what?
That something will catch fire behind the closed door,
something that's been left behind. And it would all be my fault.
A child is running around in there, burning.
No one can hear him
until I become his scream.

In 'Epilogue', which ends both *The Burning Child* and *Guarding the Air*,
the boy returns, assigned the age at which Harding wrote the poems:

And the boy wakes up.
The flames have stopped licking at the walls and roof.
The smell of smoke remains, but it comes from
the pipe that's gone out. He is sixty-two now.

The last words of *Guarding the Air* are these:

The boy sits at the kitchen table and draws.
He wants me to leave him in peace.
Later he'll come to me with the paper
and show me what he saw
in the middle of the fire.

Eric Torgersen

NOTES ON CONTRIBUTORS

MONIZA ALVI was born in Pakistan. *Homesick for the Earth*, her versions of the French-Uruguan poet Jules Supervielle, was published by Bloodaxe Books in 2011. Her most recent poetry collection *At the Time of Partition* (Bloodaxe Books, 2013) was shortlisted for the T.S. Eliot Prize. She lives in Wymondham, Norfolk where she tutors for The Poetry School.

RACHEL TZVIA BACK's collection *In the Illuminated Dark: Selected Poems of Tuvia Ruebner* was awarded the triennial TLS Risa Domb/Porjes Prize (2016) and was a finalist for both the Jewish Book Award and the National Translation Award in Poetry (2015). Back's own poetry collections include *A Messenger Comes (Elegies)*, *On Ruins & Return* and *Azimuth*.

MARIA BLOSHTEYN is the author of *The Making of a Counter-Culture Icon: Henry Miller's Dostoevsky* (University of Toronto Press, 2007) and the translator of Alexander Galich's *Dress Rehearsal: A Story in Four Acts and Five Chapters* (Slavica, 2009) and Anton Chekhov's *The Prank* (NYRB Classics, 2015).

SIDDHARTHA BOSE's books include *Kalagora, Digital Monsoon,* and *Back and Forth*. His most recent play, *No Dogs, No Indians*, had its world premiere at the Brighton Festival.

SAMPURNA CHATTARJI is a poet, novelist and translator with 14 books to her credit, the latest being *Space Gulliver: Chronicles of an Alien* (HarperCollins, 2015).

GEET CHATURVEDI is one of the most widely read contemporary Hindi authors. He has published six books, including two collections of poetry. He was awarded the Bharat Bhushan Agrawal Award for poetry and the Krishna Pratap Award for fiction. His works have been translated into seventeen languages.

ROHINI CHOWDHURY is a children's writer, and an established literary translator, with more than thirty books and several short stories to her credit. Her published writing is in Hindi and English, and covers a wide spectrum of literary genres including translations, novels, short fiction, comics, and non-fiction.

J. DEVIKA is a writer, teacher, translator, historian and interdisciplinary social-science researcher. She researches and teaches at Centre for Development Studies, Thiruvananthapuram, Kerala. Her political commentary on contemporary Kerala may be found on www.kafila.online

EDWARD DOEGAR is a Complete Works fellow and consulting editor at *The Rialto*. His pamphlet, *For Now*, has recently been published by Clinic.

BORIS DRALYUK is a literary translator and executive editor of the *Los Angeles Review of Books*. He is the editor of *1917: Stories and Poems from the Russian Revolution* (Pushkin Press, 2016), and co-editor, with Robert Chandler and Irina Mashinski, of *The Penguin Book of Russian Poetry* (2015).

NURDURAN DUMAN is a Turkish poet, editor, and translator who lives in Istanbul. *Semi Circle*, a chapbook of her poems translated into English, was published in the United States in 2016, and further translations can be found in *Asymptote, Colorado Review, Faultline, Interim* and others. She is a member of Turkish PEN and is the workshop coordinator for DAM.

KINGA FABÓ is a Hungarian poet. Her latest book, a bilingual Indonesian-English poetry collection *Racun/Poison*, was published in 2015 in Jakarta, Indonesia. Fabó's poetry has been published in international literary magazines as well as in anthologies like *The Significant Anthology, Women in War, The Colours of Refuge, Poetry Against Racism, World Poetry Yearbook 2015*.

SARABJEET GARCHA is a bilingual poet, editor and translator. He is the author of three books of poems, one of which is in Hindi, and two books of translations. *Lullaby of the Ever-Returning* (Poetrywala, 2012) is his latest collection.

JÁN GAVURA is the author of three collections, *Burning Bees* (Pálenie včiel, 2001), which was awarded the Ivan Krasko Prize for the best debut book in the Slovak language, the second *Every Morning You Are* (Každým ránom si, 2006) and his most recent collection *Besa* (2012) received a major prize from the Slovak Literary Fund.

VISHWAJYOTI GHOSH is an Indian graphic novelist and artist. He is author of the graphic novel *Delhi Calm* (2010) a political commentary remembering the state of internal emergency from 1975 to 1977, referred to in India as 'The Emergency'. His most recent book publication was as curator of the group project *This Side That Side: Restorying Partition*, an anthology of graphic narratives by 48 illustrators and authors from southern Asia.

JOHANNES GÖRANSSON has published six books of poetry, and translated six more, including four by Aase Berg. He teaches at the University of Notre Dame and edits Action Books, a press specializing in works in translation.

JOY GOSWAMI is a celebrated Bengali poet with five collected works, one verse-novel and 37 poetry titles of which *Whiplash* (Signet Press, 2017) is the latest.

GOPIKA JADEJA is a bi-lingual poet writing in English and Gujarati, and a translator.

ANN JÄDERLUND is the author of ten influential and critically acclaimed books of poetry, most recently *Djupa, kärlek, ingen: dikter 1992–2015* (*Deep, love, nobody: poems 1992–2015*).

LEELADHAR JAGOORI is a poet, teacher and journalist and the author of thirteen books of poetry in Hindi. His poems have been widely translated and published. He has received the Raghuvir Sahay Sammaan, the Sahitya Akademi Award and the Padma Shri.

VERONIKA KRASNOVA graduated from Moscow University where she studied English and American literature. She collaborated with George Szirtes and Moniza Alvi on translations from Akhmatova, Mandelstam and Tsvetaeva.

IRINA MASHINSKI is the author of nine books of poetry in Russian. She is co-editor, with Robert Chandler and Boris Dralyuk, of *The Penguin Book of Russian Poetry* (2015) and editor-in-chief of the StoSvet/Cardinal Points literary project.

KAREN MCCARTHY WOOLF has represented British writing widely, from Mexico City and Singapore to the US and the Caribbean. Her work is translated into Spanish, Swedish and Turkish. *Seasonal Disturbances* (Carcanet, 2017) is a Poetry Book Society Recommendation.

ARVIND KRISHNA MEHROTRA's most recent book, *Collected Poems*, was published by Giramondo in 2016. His translations of Vinod Kumar Shukla have appeared in *The Baffler*, *n+1* and *Granta*, and he is currently translating with Sara Rai Shukla's short fiction. He lives in Dehradun.

MONIKA KUMAR writes poetry in Hindi, and teaches British Poetry as well as Indian Writing in English at the Regional Institute of English, Chandigarh.

PHILIP MOSLEY is Distinguished Professor of English and Comparative Literature at the Pennsylvania State University, USA. He has translated several Belgian authors including François Jacqmin whose *Book of the Snow* (Arc) was shortlisted for the 2010 Griffin Poetry Prize.

DALJIT NAGRA was born to Sikh Punjabi parents and lives in West London. He has written a version of *Ramayana* (Faber & Faber) and his current collection is *British Museum* (Faber & Faber).

APURVA NARAIN is Kunwar Narain's son and translator into English, Apurva's book of translations, *No Other World*, was published in India and the UK. A second book is under way.

KUNWAR NARAIN is regarded as one of the finest living poets and a leading literary figure of India. A widely-read, reclusive presence in Hindi literature, his many honours include the *Jnanpith*, India's highest literary award across all genres and languages.

PADMA NARAYANAN is the translator of several books of literary fiction from the Tamil, most recently La. Sa. Ramamritham's *Apeetha*.

VIVEK NARAYANAN's books of poems include *Universal Beach* and *Life and Times of Mr S*. He is co-editor of the journal *Almost Island*.

BERNARD O'DONOGHUE was born in County Cork in 1945. Since 1965 he has lived in Oxford where he taught Medieval English at Wadham College. He has published seven volumes of poems, as well as a verse translation of *Sir Gawain and the Green Knight* for Penguin Classics (2006), and *Reading Chaucer's Poems* (Faber, 2015).

LEV OZEROV (1914–1996), born Lev Goldberg, was a prominent Russian-language poet and literary critic of the Soviet era. *Portraits Without Frames* will be published in an English edition, edited by Robert Chandler and Boris Dralyuk, in 2018.

K.G. SANKARA PILLAI is one of Kerala's finest poets. A recipient of the state and central Sahitya Akademi Awards in 1998 and 2002 respectively, he has authored seven volumes of poetry in Malayalam. He lives in Thrissur, Kerala.

KUTTI REVATHI is the author of nine collections of poetry in Tamil, but she is also a filmmaker, film lyricist, anthologist, editor and a doctor trained in the traditional Siddha system of medicine.

VIMMI SADARANGANI has three books of poetry and books for children to her credit. She teaches at the Tolani Arts College of Arts and Science in Adipur (Kutch), India.

TAIMOOR SHAHID's publications include *The Madness of Waiting*, a translation with critical introduction of the nineteenth-century sequel of the canonical Urdu novel *Umrao Jan Ada* (Zubaan Books India, 2013), and *The Dangerous Man*, a translation of two early twentieth-century Urdu classic novels (Random House India, 2011).

ADITYA SHANKAR writes and publishes poetry, flash fiction, and articles in leading journals across the globe. He is working towards editing a book of translations, *Tiny Judges Shall Arrive*, for AHRC, Hong Kong. His previous books include *Party Poopers* (2014) and *After Seeing* (2006).

VINOD KUMAR SHUKLA lives in Raipur, Chattisgarh, where he taught at the Indira Gandhi Agricultural University. He has published several collections of poetry and five novels, one of which, *A Window Lived in a Wall*, won the Sahitya Akademi Award.

WILL STONE is a poet, essayist and literary translator whose first poetry collection *Glaciation* (Salt, 2007), won the international Glen Dimplex Award for poetry in 2008. His third collection *The Sleepwalkers* was published by Shearsman in April 2016. Will's literary translations include works by Zweig, Roth, Betz and Rilke.

JAMES SUTHERLAND-SMITH lectures in British Cultural Studies in the Institute of English and American Studies at Prešov University. He has published six collections of poetry, the last, *Mouth*, was published by Shearsman Books (2014). He has translated a number of Slovak poets into English and received the Hviezdoslav Prize in 2003 for his translations.

AFZAL AHMED SYED is a leading voice of contemporary Urdu poetry. Born in Ghazipur, India (1946), he has lived in Karachi, Pakistan since 1976 where he works as an entomologist. An English translation of his selected poems titled *Rococo and Other Worlds* was published by Wesleyan University Press in 2010. He currently teaches at Habib University, Karachi.

GEORGE SZIRTES is a Hungarian-born poet and translator. His most recent book is *Mapping the Delta* (Bloodaxe, 2016).

ANITHA THAMPI is a Malayalam poet with three collections of poetry to her credit. Her work has been translated into English, French, German, Swedish as well as various Indian languages. She is also the translator of Les Murray, Carlo Collodi and Juan Ramón Jiménez and Mourid Barghouti.

RÓISÍN TIERNEY taught for several years in Spain (Valladolid and Granada), and now lives in London. Her pamphlet *Dream Endings* (Rack Press) won the 2012 Michael Marks Award. Her collection *The Spanish-Italian Border* is published by Arc.

ERIC TORGERSEN's latest collection is *In Which We See Our Selves: American Ghazals*, Mayapple Press, 2017. He also translates Rilke and Nicolas Born.

FRANCISCO FERNÁNDEZ TORRES lives in Granada, Spain. He has published two collections of poetry and is currently working on his third. He is an habitué of Miguel's Tavern.

GUY VAES (1927–2012) was a Belgian author whose magic realist fiction also drew on modernist psychological investigation and on existentialist ideas of alienation. An accomplished photographer, Vaes was also a film critic for the Brussels magazine *Spécial*, and his reviews were published in 2007 as *111 Films: chroniques de cinema (1970–1983)*.